THE **GENEROUS EXCHANGE**

How Attention to Beauty, Goodness and Excellence Restores Us and Our World

MARIA SIROIS, PSY.D.

Cover image by Simon D'Entremont
Cover and page design by by Anna Myers Sabatini

Green Fire Press
PO Box 377 Housatonic MA 01236

Publisher's Cataloging-in-Publication Data

Names: Sirois, Maria, author.
Title: The generous exchange : how attention to beauty, goodness and excellence restores us and our world / Maria Sirois, Psy.D.
Description: Includes bibliographical references. | Housatonic, MA: Green Fire Press, 2025.
Identifiers: LCCN: 2024927047 | ISBN: 979-8-9899452-3-8 (paperback) | 979-8-9899452-4-5 (ebook)
Subjects: LCSH Aesthetics–Psychological aspects. | Aesthetics. | Virtue. | Environmental psychology. | Self-actualization (Psychology) | Self-management (Psychology) | Self help. | Essays. | BISAC PSYCHOLOGY / Environmental Psychology | PSYCHOLOGY / Essays | SELF-HELP / Motivational & Inspirational | SCIENCE / Essays | PHILOSOPHY / Essays | PHILOSOPHY / Mind & Body | PHILOSOPHY / Aesthetics
Classification: LCC BF637.S4 S57 2025 | DDC 158.1—dc23

Praise for *The Generous Exchange*

"Sometimes, the world feels dark, scary, and overbearing; we may keep our heads down, afraid to glimpse one more heartbreaking failure of our kind to live decently. Some days, we don't want to attract the wrath of others, and we can't bear to absorb more of others' pain. When we cringe from the shadows, the madmen, or the ghosts of our own past, we shrink the world we live in, and ourselves to fit in it. Maria Sirois' book *The Generous Exchange* coaxes us to raise our heads again. Beauty and excellence draw us out and up into the best of the world, the best of each other. In carefully chosen, and beautifully assembled stories, quotes, and revelations, *The Generous Exchange* works on the reader the way a break in the clouds fills with a beam of golden light. Reading this book is like gazing at the illuminated vision lit by that beam. We see and appreciate details, the magnified greatness of that tree or hillside or little lake. But the beam itself beckons, like a bridge from the ground we tread to something spectacular above us. Suddenly we don't just live in a flat, bleak world, we also live in the heavens. This was the feeling consistently evoked for me as I read this treasure—that by widening our eyes to beauty and excellence, by gathering courage or strength or heart from them, though we may walk the same paths through our days, the world we travel through becomes more extraordinary—a place truly worth cherishing."

—Michael F. Steger, Ph.D., Director of the Center for Meaning and Purpose, Colorado State University

"*The Generous Exchange: How Attention to Beauty, Goodness and Excellence Restores Us and Our World* is more than just a book; it's an experience that invites us to see life through fresh eyes and an open heart. In a world that feels broken and overwhelming, this book is a much-needed balm, reminding us of the beauty and goodness that still exists all around us—and within us. Through a provocative blend

I

of stories, research, and reflection, Dr. Sirois shows how the simple act of noticing can transform the ordinary into the extraordinary, grounding us in the present and renewing our hope in life's resilience. What I appreciate most, however, is that *The Generous Exchange* does more than inspire appreciation; it invites us to action. Dr. Sirois makes a powerful case for becoming stewards of beauty and goodness, urging us to let our love for what is beautiful and good guide us toward compassion, kindness, and deeper connections. It's a moving reminder that when we protect and celebrate beauty, we find purpose and meaning—and even healing. Reading this book reshaped how I perceive the world and my role in it. It guided me to revisit my life with fresh, appreciative eyes and inspired me to make the pursuit of beauty and goodness a daily practice. I have no doubt that everyone who reads this book will feel more connected, grateful, and inspired to uncover and cultivate beauty in every moment."

—Lindsey N. Godwin, Ph.D., author, practitioner, possibilitizer; Academic Director, David L. Cooperrider Center for Appreciative Inquiry, Champlain College

"Maria's writing, with her careful choice of words and deliberate turns of phrase, reaches deep within us. There is no hint of arrogance in her mastery of the written word; instead, there is a natural beauty that speaks to the reader, befriends you, sees you, and nourishes you. I sincerely believe that each reader will become wiser and richer (in the truest sense of the word) by absorbing and integrating this delightful book. Whether it significantly helps heal our world is now up to us. Guided by Maria's wisdom, I will do my best to contribute."

—Justin Robinson, Director, The Wellbeing Distillery

"As the vulnerabilities of our world become more prevalent and real and our sense of optimism is compromised, *The Generous Exchange* emerges as both a beacon of hope and a call to action. Maria Sirois offers us a beautiful gift as she invites us to explore the power of appreciating natural beauty, moral goodness and excellence as a way of igniting positive change within us and throughout our wounded world. As an author, Maria shares a tapestry of her own personal stories, and the stories of others, to illustrate everyday, often simple moments of clarity that lend themselves to a heightened understanding and recognition of beauty, goodness and excellence. She grounds these stories in research and insightful wisdom that further inspires us to embrace these important moments as a practice or ritual of appreciation and reflection that will lead to a more compassionate and unified world."

—Molly McGuigan, transformational change consultant, appreciative inquiry expert, co-author, *Ditch the Ditty*

"Maria Sirois is a healer of people and communities, and when she turns her attention and voice to healing our global village, I feel more optimistic about what lies ahead. This profound book is a gift to you and to our shared future."

—Tal Ben-Shahar, Ph.D., cofounder, Happiness Studies Academy, author of *Happier, No Matter What*

"In times of growing fragmentation, chaos, violence, and uncertainty, the fundamental question of how we live our lives has become more crucial than ever. With remarkable insight and inspiration, Maria Sirois delves into the enduring qualities that form the essence of our human experience—spirituality, vulnerability, wonder, imagination, love, creativity, beauty, goodness, and excellence. She skillfully identifies these elements as the delicate yet powerful ingredients that have the potential to reconnect us with the profound, mysterious, and awe-inspiring experience of being fully and meaningfully alive. I wholeheartedly recommend this book as a treasure trove of profound wisdom and captivating beauty. It stands as a testament to the enduring power of human goodness and serves as a much-needed beacon of hope and light in our challenging world."

—Dr. Pninit Russo-Netzer, Ph.D., researcher, leading speaker, author; head of the Compass Institute for the Study and Application of Meaning in Life, and the Resilience and Optimal Development Lab, Achva Academic College

"Although engaging with beauty involves sensory/perceptual systems, and knowledge/meaning systems, it is primarily about the heart—and this book is full of heart. It moved me deeply and I resonated to it with awe."

—Rhett Diessner, Ph.D., Professor Emeritus of Psychology, Lewis-Clark State College; author, *Understanding the Beauty Appreciation Trait: Empirical Research on Seeking Beauty in All Things*

"Maria Sirois's words, stories, quotes, and practices will lift you. Reading her book will give you an appreciation you may have known existed—but didn't know how to attain. Let Maria lead you on a journey of inner and outer discovery. There is no better guide to beauty, goodness, and excellence."

—Dan Tomasulo, Ph.D., Academic Director, Spirituality Mind Body Institute, Columbia University, author of *Learned Hopefulness*

THE **GENEROUS EXCHANGE**

How Attention to Beauty, Goodness and
Excellence Restores Us and Our World

MARIA SIROIS, PSY.D.

 Green
Fire
Press

Housatonic
Massachusetts

For those who cared for the Earth and
its creatures long before our time,
for those who care now,
and those yet to come.

THE GENEROUS EXCHANGE
Contents

Foreword

I see great beauty in the stingray as he glides along the ocean bottom like an angel of the sea. I see beauty in one wolf spider that has magically appeared in my basement now staring at me inside a glass cup turned over on her. I cherish the beauty of my child's smiling energy as she rushes to tell me something about her new drawing. I hear the beauty of the booming thunder as it overshadows the pattering of rain on my roof above. These experiences initiate a turn in me. They point me toward life that is all around me. It is life waiting for me to connect to it. As I write this, I feel gratitude for this strength of appreciation of beauty—it is something Maria and I share as a signature strength—as its fresh force empowers me out of my head and into the world.

You know how movie experts will sometimes refer to the movie's "setting" as a character? This means the entire setting where the movie unfolds is important enough to be called out alongside the actual characters in the movie. I view this book similarly—it is a character in and of itself. Yes, there is, within it, prose and poetry. Stories and practices. But there is a whole character here too. A character that is real and deeply authentic. It evokes a lot of feelings and you, the reader, will empathize and feel deeply. It *will* impact you, if you are open. And, this character is the poetry in the stories and it is the practices within the poetry, the prose within the practices. This is one of Maria's gifts: she creates an interbeing across the pages—an interdependence of everything within the book itself. Perhaps she is embodying and then reflecting back our own interdependence as a human species with all of life on the planet?

The book's foundation is Maria's depths and also the psychological science. Science informs us that the character strength of appreciation of beauty matters, a lot. It is the most important strength, by far, for our connection and relationship with nature. Whether you relate to nature and our planet by creating meaning, engaging your senses, opening to your emotions, or experiencing compassion for animals, trees, and rivers, it is the appreciation of beauty strength that offers a strong pathway. It is this strength that is more connected than any other strength to predicting whether we will follow one of our core callings as human beings and take action to be good stewards for the environment. Related, this strength is linked strongly with the form of mindfulness known as acting with awareness. And, appreciation of beauty is the grease for our emotion of elevation. Elevation occurs when we are motivated to do good and be kind after we observe the character strengths and caring acts of others. This strength can impact ourselves and our world.

This is the landscape of Maria's book. You have the opportunity to read and be elevated and this might then *cause* you to do more good in the world. That is a healing opportunity.

Often when I read Maria's books, I am awash with insight, lost in a story, or simply happy to be here, reading. I then wonder about the how of her writing and I imagine she is writing from her brilliant mind, and then I think she is writing from her gracious heart, and then I think it is coming from her wise soul. I soon realize, (again), she is doing all of these at the same time. Somehow, she does this. And here, she does it with a topic that is universal and spiritual and meaningful for all of us.

It is beauty.

—**Ryan M. Niemiec, Psy.D.,** Chief Science & Education Officer, VIA Institute on Character, author of *Mindfulness and Character Strengths; The Power of Character Strengths*; and *Peace Psychology and Character Strengths*.

Introduction

During the dark, dank days of the pandemic, when so much moldered in the fear of a virus gone mad and so much died, I found myself in a moment of exhaustion. Not only a physical fatigue, but an emotional weariness I had only known in one other time—the time of my brother's death and the dissolution of my marriage. Then, I wondered at the point of it all—why bother to live when something so alive as a baby brother could die within a ten-week span and a marriage dissolve despite decades of care?

In this more recent exhaustion, brought on by overwork and pandemic chaos, I began to feel as though nothing I had ever done would ever add up to anything of merit. All that I had fought for as a young woman—justice, equality, abortion rights, marital rights—was at risk. And all I had striven for as a professional—the building of resilient capacity within human beings—seemed Sisyphean.

Rates of depression, anxiety and suicidality were on the increase across all ages, and for the first time in my life happiness seemed not only unattainable, but an unworthy pursuit.

Why seek joy or pleasure or delight when the world burned?

Why bother adding one more slide to my teachings or one more signature to a protest letter when the waves of the times appeared to be contrary, life-destroying, and incomprehensible to my soul?

I entered 2021 with one commitment: to find a way back to myself, to a meaning that made sense. But first I would have to bring some energy into my body; to literally infuse my bones with enough vitality to want to keep showing up for life.

Carl Jung once wrote that "to penetrate the darkness, we must summon all the powers of enlightenment that consciousness can offer." I was on a simpler quest: "What might be a moment in a day to look forward to, that would draw me out from beneath covers of my bed and entice me to enter that day?"

I experimented with three things: 1) a daily diary in which I wrote one true thing to myself, one honest reflection of what I was thinking and feeling that I would never say out loud; 2) exercise two times a week; and 3) a commitment to find one story of beauty or goodness or excellence that I would write about once a month.

One truth, one story, two workouts.

The truth diary lasted a few months and was pure deliciousness; it was just so powerful to admit how sad I was or how angry, frustrated or hopeless, without having to justify my feelings to anyone. I acknowledged how it pisses me off that people don't RSVP to invitations. Or how annoying it is to raise a child who can't make a meal, only to realize that this is on me for failing to drag them into the kitchen at any point during all those mothering years.

Exercise reminded me of who I have been my entire life: the 3-year-old child my father nicknamed Monkeyface for how often he caught me climbing (trees, bookcases, fences); the young adult slapping the ball on the field hockey field; the middle-aged woman learning soccer and pickleball and once, only once, getting back on the golf course; something I had avoided since my eighth-grade year when my father tried valiantly to shape my drive into something worthy of play.

But the beauty work, that once-a-month assignment I had given myself, became so much more than the Red Bull energy boost I had been seeking. It became a lifeline, *the* lifeline tethering me to living.

Beauty awakens. We know this as we experience the awe evidenced in the body tremors of a four-year-old, who, upon seeing dolphins crest the ocean waves along the Miami shore, turns toward us in delight, but cannot not speak. All the words of his exclamative, exuberant vocabulary inadequate to express his astonishment in the presence of a sea creature's leaping play.

Beauty heals. How many of us find consolation in the daily walks we take in our neighborhoods, struck by the flash of blue in the jay or the pink of the azalea, colors and sights seen and barely registered during more "normal" times, but now, after the smog of Covid, appearing as a balm, a gift of natural living that carries within it a tiny but powerful promise: that despite our massive messing up of so much, life finds a way to continue on.

Beauty inspires our better selves. We protect what we find beautiful. We nourish moral beauty—goodness—by allowing ourselves to be moved and then motivated to be equally good, becoming one in cycles of generosity. We are kinder, love more easily, and are gentler in the presence of beautiful souls offering the best of themselves to the world through art, dance, language, science, exploration. We don't destroy or ignore or demean splendor; we elevate it when and how we can and are moved to bring others into its sphere.

And, in the most inspiring of research, we have discovered that the appreciation of beauty in its natural forms, as well as in its moral form—the beauty of the human heart—catalyzes positive behavior toward our world. It arouses positive emotions *and* action. We are kinder toward each other and toward the land itself (Diessner & Niemiec, 2022).[1]

Month by month I returned to myself. I collected stories, anecdotes and images that pointed to goodness, excellence and loveliness within and around us. I noted what the exemplars of morality were doing while I rested in the chair off the back deck and watched the white-tail deer travel the same path day in and day out to nibble at our grasses, surprised again to see how still they hold when startled and how easefully they return to the present moment as danger passes. I researched how and why beauty matters and found a depth of science that not only points toward its impact on any one soul but its importance in the very future of our living; for you see, if we cannot find beauty in each other or in the natural kingdoms that compose our planet we will fail to do what we must to keep the planet alive.

Bit by bit, story by story, vista by vista, I returned to life.

In offering this work I hope to inspire you to remember your place in the community of things. I offer a reminder to care for that which you find beautiful; an encouragement to hold dear the wonder of life on this planet and, as you do so, to deepen your commitment to make certain that that wonder holds for future generations. To consider participating just a bit more actively in a generous exchange with life itself and its beings.

We have ruined so much. So much is still possible. Both are true.

Love,
Maria

An Important Note About this Book:

The Character Strength of Appreciation of Beauty and Excellence

A central premise of this work is that we benefit when we activate the specific character strength of *Appreciation of Beauty and Excellence*. This strength refers to three aspects worthy of appreciation: appreciation of natural beauty, of moral beauty (also known as moral goodness), and of excellence.

As described in the handbook of character strengths and virtues,[2] a compilation of the 24 character strengths determined by leading psychologists to represent the best of humanity, "Appreciation of Beauty and Excellence...refers to the ability to find, recognize and take pleasure in the existence of goodness in the physical and social worlds. A person high in this strength frequently feels awe and related emotions (including admiration, wonder, and elevation) while, for example, walking in the woods or in a city, while reading novels or newspapers, while learning about other people's lives or while watching sports or movies." The strength is known to provide benefit to the person activating any of the three forms of appreciation, and to provide value to those of us who witness or receive that appreciation.

Throughout this book, I have tried to capture how appreciation of beauty and excellence may show up in any one day, and how that kind of appreciation changes us. It builds our sense of hopefulness and resilience and ignites our potential contribution to the climate distress that haunts us. I reflect as well on the value of the strength through the research that supports this character quality as a crucial underpinning of our wellbeing. I offer research to ground this work beyond this moment, so that you may come to see that it isn't just within our lives that the activation of this strength matters, it will matter dearly in the lives of those who come after us.

An appreciative gaze enhances our lives. And it may help us find ways to actively protect our world. To that end, I have included a section on how to practice this strength for yourself, for the young ones under your care, and in relationship to those you love.

Beauty, goodness, excellence—our world is replete with them—and should we wish to steward this world so that those to come experience them as well, then it behooves us to pause, notice, savor and elevate them wherever and whenever we can.

SECTION ONE

Beauty

"Frequently, beauty is playful like dancing sunlight, it cannot be predicted...Without intending it, we find ourselves coming alive with a sense of celebration and delight. The pedestrian sequence of a working day breaks, a new door opens and the heart recognizes the silent majesty of the ordinary."

—John O'Donohue

The Promise of Beauty

"Beauty might just be the thing to enable our wholeness."

—Rhett Diessner

Yesterday I lost three hours to a malware issue on my laptop; one in which I demonstrated an astonishing naivete by listening to supposed tech repair people (also known as scammers) talk me through an elaborate process to "protect all my data from the consequences of the obvious identity theft that was in process."

My vulnerability to this sort of thing appears every few decades or so. Like the time I listened to a phone call from an "IRS" representative telling me I needed legal representation for a failure to pay back taxes—before I knew that the IRS never calls you, just like I know now that Microsoft and Apple care nothing for your travel habits and anyone who queries you about them as supposed Apple tech care people is not legit.

The three hours lost in the maze of determining what was real and what wasn't was nothing compared to the seven hours following in which I found myself walking aimlessly through the house, unable to concentrate, shocked again at our ability to be cruel to one another.

We live in a fragmented time. Read any paper, listen to any news station and there is more than enough evidence to support a belief in the disintegration of the values and decency that we long for in our civilizations. Leadership consultant

Margaret Wheatley asks for a return to sanity in her recent book *Restoring Sanity*[3], citing a perfect storm of greed, fear, and climate-related catastrophes. In August, 2023 *New York Times* columnist David Brooks bemoaned the crisis of immaturity across the United States, arguing that "the instability of the self has created an immature public culture—impulsive, dramatic, erratic and cruel. In institution after institution, from churches to schools to nonprofits, the least mature voices dominate and hurl accusations, while the most mature lie low, trying to get through the day."

We are assaulted, insulted and battered by strain.

Consider if you will, the conversations we are not having at the bus stop or the grocery line. We are not talking about the evidence of generosity across the globe, or the success of micro-investing initiatives to development financial acumen and stability in regions far from the Global North. We do not celebrate progress made in the re-introduction of species to the wild, and no one in any circle I know has bothered to call me up to ask, "What's the best thing you've seen in your travels across the continents?" We discuss the horror of the day or the reality show headline. We dread upcoming elections and gird ourselves for battle while pummeling ourselves internally for what we haven't figured out yet about women's rights to their bodies, long-term marriages, racism, violence, famine, body appreciation, raising children, men's health, supporting young adults, supporting elders, and balancing work and home.

Against this assault, what value beauty? If truly, "nothing gold can stay," what is the point of noting the gold against a backdrop of hurricane-force devastation?

The answer, I believe, can be found in the smallest moments of our own histories.

~~~

9/14/2001: Three days after 9/11. I take my children out to a local park. We are waiting for their father to return home—he had been visiting family in Long Island and had stayed to see how he might be of help. We are holding our breaths for the aftershocks—who else has died? How many are still missing? Who haven't we heard from? What else is in store? I've sent money to the Red Cross, as well as to my Aunt Theresa, who is furiously knitting booties for the rescue dogs whose paws are being burned in the ashes. I've sent messages to the parents at my children's elementary school about resilience. The waiting itself has become a force in our home - a barometric pressure bomb of a storm; each time the phone rings I jump.

When the waiting evolves into a tornado of tortuous facts, I take my children to the park with the tiny creek, hosting the smallest of fish, where they can toddle in water up to their ankles and listen to the sounds of autumn in New England: the calling of birds, the chirping of crickets, the rustle of leaves and the creaking of branches. In our tiny oasis, my children are safe and I notice that I am breathing. That is all. I am not healed or uplifted yet; a windstorm of hate and grief shreds the air around us on the East Coast. But at the creek, with my children running and swinging and oohing at fish, I can take a breath without panic and that is the beginning of the beginning of an eventual recovery.

~~~

5/13/17: The phone rings at 5 a.m. I am in Geneva, New York for my daughter's college graduation. We are headed that morning to an award ceremony where she will be acknowledged, and then a day of packing, lunching, and cheering her onward, until her Commencement ceremony the next morning. The day is misty with sun peeking among clouds now and then, and I watch this powerful star—our Sun—carefully, until her radiance breaks forth in the afternoon. I choose a space between my ex-husband, my boyfriend and my son during meals so that I can see my daughter and have my face in the path of the sun at the same time. All day long, I seek the orb's glow, for just that morning, on that 5 a.m. call, I learned that my father died peacefully in the middle of the night. I want to celebrate my daughter and I feel deeply the pull of reaching toward my father and in the tension of the two, the one thing that enables me to hold both, is the sun. I am not thinking. I am not analyzing, philosophizing or psychologizing. I am drawn, as if in undertow, back and again to the sun.

"Nature itself is the best physician," wrote Hippocrates, and on the day I lost my father, I knew that to be true.

Why bother valuing beauty? Because it provides a pathway to health, happiness and wholeness. As described by many researchers (notably Capaldi & Passmore),[4] the benefits of connecting with nature include an increased sense of purpose and connectedness to oneself and to the world, as well as an increase in the sense of autonomy, authenticity, and overall wellbeing and satisfaction.

In 2016, *Time Magazine* published research about nature as a source of healing, citing a study by Yoshifumi Miyazaki, a forest-therapy expert and researcher at Chiba University in Japan.[5] Miyazaki ad discovered that people who spent at least 40 minutes walking in a cedar forest showed lower levels of cortisol, a hormone related to both blood pressure and immune system function which is known to be elevated under stress. "Spending time in the forest induces a state of physiologic relaxation," Miyazaki said.

Growing bodies of research in the last decade have demonstrated the positive effects of nature engagement relative to anxiety, self-esteem, mood regulation, experiences of loneliness, nervous system arousal and cognitive function, elevation of positive emotions and a sense of meaning. When we experience nature, we are calmed, relieved, elevated and aroused in all the good ways, and because of this we may find our way to wholeness—wholeness as a sense of health, and also as a sense of integration, a sense of things making sense, of cohering, if only for a time.

I think, too, of the work of Dr. Lucy Hone, resilient grieving expert, who has written extensively about the importance of asking oneself, as one begins the life-long work of integrating the pain of loss, "Is what I am doing helping or harming me?"

So often, as a psychologist working in the territory of loss, I have invited parents who have lost a child to consider, "Where are you most at peace?" This question is meant to help them notice what works to provide them with a temporary easing of their grief. Sometimes they will point to a place of quiet, such as a temple or a meditation mat. Others will name a ritual moment: lying in bed with music playing on Sundays or morning tea with a friend. So often, in those first weeks and months after a child has died, parents will tell me that they find peace in nature: in their garden or hiking in the hills; listening to the birds singing outside the window; or watching the light in the sky change and seeing the stars come out.

In nature, we are soothed.

The promise of beauty in nature is not that all will be completely well or that the blights on our planet will disappear. Rather, in appreciating nature's splendor, we may find ourselves beyond ourselves for an instant and in this bypass of a self-oriented focus on our pain, discover a vitality within that has not yet been dampened. We are, for that moment, enabled to continue on.

A Bend in the Light

"A thing of beauty is a joy forever: its loveliness increases; it will never pass into nothingness."

—John Keats

One morning, unable to sleep, I went to stand on the stairs at the Kripalu retreat center, overlooking the great lawn that slopes down to the lake. It was perhaps 5 a.m. and a few other non-sleepers were standing there as well. We stood apart from each other, granting a private distance, and held silent, at the edge of the stairs, just where the lawn begins. Perhaps, like me, they just couldn't sleep. Or perhaps they felt a pull to liminal moments when light floods the land, and the promise of dawn is known. "It is possible," I remember thinking that morning, "that some people wake to greet the day at the literal crack of dawn without grumble. That might be a thing."

As we stood that spring morning, I took in the early flowers, the green of a grass alive with loving care and dew, the trees budded and trembling with hope, and a pervasive calm—one sweetened with the smallest of bird song. The sky began to show itself, clouds lifting from the top of the lake so slowly as to have been pulled by the oldest of curtain pullers at a theater, one tender inch at a time. In the stillness, bunnies began to nibble the grasses near our feet. This cannot happen unless you are so quiet that they feel safe and, in that safety, free.

The clouds lifted, the bunnies sniffed and chewed, the birds sang, and in a surprising shift, something happened to the sky.

19

There must have been a bend in the light for suddenly every-thing flushed with pink. We couldn't yet see the sun—she still hid beneath our horizon but all that surrounded the land was cast in a pink the shade of a shell and between the bunnies and the quiet and the pink, my eyes began to water and in the water-ing, everything blurred some, and with that blurring and the fullness of a dawn coming toward us with such benevolence I found myself thinking, "This is how Monet saw the world, this is what Monet saw," a world flush with a blend of color and light and vibrancy so exquisite as to make one's eyes water with tears.

Now, even in the remembering from eight years distance—eight years of the normal cracking of a life—I feel as blessed by the memory as I felt that morning. As if I had been invited and welcomed and known.

To find beauty we must be still. To hold onto beauty, to have it become a thrum of our living, to have it inform who we are enough so that beauty becomes the offering of our soul, we have to be willing to revere its presence. To not simply gaze and exclaim but to bring such a deep sense of attention that we feel seen by the very element upon which we have cast our gaze. The light bent. Pink swaddled us in an embrace no less powerful than the encirclement of a small child's arm around her father's neck.

There is a psychological understanding in infant develop-ment that the healthiest caregivers know to hold a baby tight enough so that the child feels secure, and loosely enough that they can lift their gaze and know the world through their own eyes. In that balanced embrace, they are both grounded and free. This is what the glow of that morning offered—an encirclement of light enough to open the world to us and defined enough to ground us right exactly there.

The land enfolded us as we beheld it and in that, we touched a kind of amity.

That the felt experience of beauty and love is often connected to the land is no surprise. When we become present to the terrains of our living—the forests and mountaintops, the oceans, rivers and lakes, along with the flora and fauna that call each place home—a visual stimulation is triggered that necessarily brings an awareness of something that is clearly larger than us, and at the same time somehow directly available to us. We cannot live without noticing, at least now and then, that the context of our living requires attention to the land we have been placed upon. On the best of days we go beyond that noticing and begin to inquire how it is possible that so much variety of life is here for us to examine, explore, play with, and learn from.

John Muir points us toward the ever-present nature of nature: "This grand show is eternal. It is always sunrise somewhere; the dew is never all dried at once; a shower is forever falling; vapor is ever rising. Eternal sunrise, eternal sunset, eternal dawn and gloaming, on sea and continents and islands, each in its turn, as the round earth rolls."

Annie Dillard reminds us in *Pilgrim at Tinker Creek*[6] of the aliveness often granted to us by the ordinary moments in that relentless rolling: "Today is one of those excellent January partly cloudies in which light chooses an unexpected part of the landscape to trick out in gilt, and then the shadow sweeps it away. You know you're alive. You take huge steps, trying to feel the planet's roundness arc between your feet."

We decide to be informed by the cloud shifts or the falling rains. We choose to let the land say something to us or represent a kind of significance to us. Even in the most urban of landscapes, terrain is available to us for discovery. Remember how the streets of Italy and Spain, lined with terraced apartments each with its own small balcony, became rivers of love in 2020, each evening offering a chorus of song to soften our loneliness. As we watched and listened, the balconies and the curving cobblestoned streets became no less a source of nourishment than the grand coursing waterways upon which ancient cities found sustenance.

We can see, really see, and notice how the landscapes right in front of us offer lessons and loveliness and illumination… or not.

We, the four of us early risers at Kripalu, stood for a few moments. The pink shifted into pale yellow tones, the sun rose fully, the bunnies began to hide and we could hear the stirrings of more retreat guests awakening to the day. I marked the spot, standing stock still and noticing where I was in relation to the stairs and the top of the lawn so that I might come back at any time and be brought back into the fold of that moment.

In the eight intervening years till now, I have visited that spot many times and nothing has happened that even comes close to the grace of that one April morning. Fair enough—I haven't actually gotten myself out of bed at 4 a.m. to be received by the exact time of rising dawn, but I have been there in early mornings and late afternoons to open myself to the land and lake and trees and bunnies and nonetheless, that moment was of itself. Irreplaceable. Impossible to replicate.

But here is the thing: I continue to be held by that moment. I continue to see the world as Monet saw it, literally from that morning on.

Maybe we don't need a thousand moments of beauty and grace to cascade upon our lives. Maybe sometimes one right moment, captured in one still heart, can be enough—can be that which changes so much. For you see, because I now often see the world through eyes that are watered with gratitude and laced with pink, I cannot see only darkness. The misery that surrounds me—and there is plenty even in my small village—does not overwhelm. We have it all—racial injustice, food insecurity, unhoused couples at the intersection of our Marshalls and grocery store plaza. Children battered, insufficient tolerance for refugees and a depressingly steady parade of abandoned and abused animals. We are no different here than anywhere.

But beauty existed once here and so it exists always.

The Concealed Beauty
of Small Moments

*"When we approach with reverence, great things decide to
approach us. Our real life comes to the surface and its light
awakens the concealed beauty in things."*

—John O'Donohue

By the curved bay at the edge of the Italian Ligurian Sea, where the brightly colored buildings of Santa Margherita greet the tourists who come to rest there, Francesca (our guide on a week-long walking tour) explained to us that many of Italians born in the 1990s and 2000s will never own a home. They live in apartments or remain with their parents, finding work as they can, saving their funds not for clothes or cars or things but rather for moments: moments with friends over dinner, or out listening to the music of the *piazza*—a symphony of glasses clinking, and matches struck and friends calling out to each other. Italy, so fully rooted in its legacy of formal beauty in art and architecture and song, reveals a more subtle beauty, one born not out of the decades of post-World War II strife (economies failing, dukedoms fading, politicians in constant battle, floods of refugees and the tragedy of more than 170,000 deaths from Covid); rather, the more subtle and ancient beauty of two people sitting by the sea, espressos in hand, watching the world pass, speaking of the small and the big things.

I first came to Italy in 1976, during the summer between my junior and senior years of high school. I had been placed as a foreign exchange student in Potenza, a rather large city in the ankle of the country's boot, living with a middle-aged couple. They had no children and brought me over, I believe, as a friend for their niece, whose parents owned a trattoria. Our evening adventure was to walk arm in arm through the town square at night, chattering about what we saw, who we saw with whom, who was ill, the latest movie release—about nothing really and somehow about everything. It felt familiar to me, with my small-town upbringing, and I remember at 16 often feeling bored. But now, at 61, sitting with Francesca over breakfast, I could sense the thrum of something important in our choice to invest in time spent together without rush or agenda or profound "big" meaning.

For a week's time, as we traveled with Francesca up the coast on our holiday, no one was alone. No one was staring at a computer for six hours straight or rushing from one patient exam room to the next. No one was hurrying to get to the gas station, to get to class, or to their second job. Each day we were hiking, 16 of us, through some of the most glorious landscapes in our world: lands with terraced olive gardens, and vineyards, abundant vegetable plants and flowers, cascading down to a brilliant blue bay. Brightly painted houses and stone statues graced every corner, and in the presence of such obvious beauty we reveled each day in the joy of having someone to walk with, and sit with, and get to know just a little bit more than the day before. Our pandemic strains brought us to the place it seems that Italians have known for hundreds of years—that place where what matters most is the chance to be together in the thick of life.

We are hungry for beauty—for the bend of the beach into a sea that is rarely cold, for the rise of the mountains against acres of vines, planted first in the 1500s. But we hunger, too, for companionship and the concealed beauty of sweetness that comes from those unpretentious shared coffees.

Sitting with Francesca, learning of her sisters and her apartment, the white walls and the small closet, the terror of living abates. Nothing is being solved—just offered. Nothing is being measured or challenged—time is full and abundant, feeling like a friend for a change. A biscotti, a warm café, a person nearby, breathing in and out together, an unfussy afternoon. This humble shared experience with its aura of kindness keeps so much of the chaos at bay—the disarray of drowning loneliness, or the scythes of fear that accompany all the larger choices in life.

It is in this remembering that I find myself wondering, might we consider a focused attention not only upon the greenery around us, or the kingdoms of furry and winged species, but also upon the beauty of small moments of connection? Might we not include them in the lens of our appreciation such that they become one of the elements that trigger awe, inspiration, mattering—just as a stunning murmuration of starlings might?

"Beauty often starts with something small," writes Cody Delistraty in his article in *The Atlantic* on "The Beauty-Happiness Connection."[7] He references a Monet painting, "Le Dejeuner," depicting lunch in a country home: a teapot, a glass, a bowl of fruit, a child nearby and a woman walking past. He suggests it is beautiful because of its very mundanity and then reminds us that when we find beauty in the ordinary, we become happier. Remembering my moments with Francesca,

I am aware of the happiness and sweetness that such ordinary moments afford.

We are not speaking now of the beauty of gorgeousness. Not the striking blaze of a rare wonder. But a beauty of merit nonetheless, for at the end of life it is these moments we recall and long for. When the rush of all the large agendas has disappeared, when so much has been resolved and so little is still possible, when our capacities are fading and our living restricted, we are brought back to the longings we each had as children. "Mommy, come play with me," becomes, "Please just come be with me." The splendor of companionship, of not aloneness, of lunch or a walk or a sit together, was and is more than enough. And when, before those final years, we can find within ourselves an appreciation for these tiny moments, we become glad for our living.

This is not only true for those of us of more advanced ages. Just a few months ago I asked my son, age 23, what he felt had been the most meaningful moments between us. I wanted to understand how my mothering mattered to him. I assumed he would mention the various trips I had taken him on, to show him the larger world and introduce him to both bigger vistas and grand thinkers in the domains he cared most about. I thought he might mention how tenacious and consistent I had been in getting my butt to every soccer match, lacrosse game, school presentation, field trip and special luncheon I possibly could. Instead, he surprised me by saying, "It was when we were both on the couch and I had my head in your lap and we watched Star Wars or Marvel stuff together."

What he said is consistent with the research about happiness in life: happiness arises from our ability to savor the small moments. I suggest there is beauty here, too, in the allure of the simple goodness of a moment.

The possibility of such moments is amplified when we begin to see ourselves as connected to others, including those from other natural kingdoms. If I were to see a pair of otters at play, my smile would light the day. If I were to notice with gratitude the sharing of touch between a momma dog and the stray kittens she has adopted, my heart would be full. We can choose to approach any moment with reverence, to see, truly see, the loveliness of a granddaughter's side-by-side walk with her grandfather, or the grace of two friends, laughing at little nothings over coffee.

The concealment, to bring us back to the wisdom of John O'Donohue, is that we often fail to honor the delight of brushing a child's hair, the sudden quick smile of a friend who we run into between the bread and cereal aisles, the wave of the neighbor we pass each morning on the way to work, or the boy, content in his pajamas, re-watching for the millionth time the lightsaber battle between Luke and the enemy of the day, allowing his mom to hold his hand and rub his head on the couch, in the den near the deck, where the cherry blossoms bloom white and pink each spring.

Some Kind of Little Contour

"Let the rain kiss you. Let the rain beat upon your head with silver liquid drops. Let the rain sing you a lullaby."

—*Langston Hughes*

In December 2021, I was helping my son pack up his apartment after he had finished college. We had many hours to chat while deciding exactly how many of the single socks we were going to hold onto vs. throw away or make into a mismatched pair. We touched on the confusing pandemic booster-shot recommendations, the general disappointment throughout the land about the lack of rapid test availability, the misunderstandings about immunity in general (he had studied bio-medical science and so has *lots* of opinions about all of this) and inevitably the failure of leadership to do the right things for our climate and the Earth. My son, generally a sunny person, had become discouraged and often distrusting of the powers that be. He can be critical, often passionately so, and quick to point to the failures of corrupt adults. I remind myself that young adulthood is often a time of sweeping negativity—there is so much fear, anxiety, uncertainty and clarity about the lack of reliable structures to support us in stabilizing our lives. His views are not isolated—distrust is rampant on college campuses. Young people, ages 18-29, face the highest levels of depression and anxiety since World War II and globally suicidality in this age group is high and rising.

This is not a time for delusional beliefs in the goodness of all things, or for a kind of blind faith that all will be well. Most of us have no idea how the future will unfold. A constant refrain plays in the back of my mind, even as we sort out the notebooks he will keep or trash or recycle. If I buy a hybrid vehicle does that make enough of a difference, given that I often fly for work? Should I care about such things when there are children in my town with food insecurity? Should I be protesting deforestation more loudly? The truth of the matter is that we all ought to be addressing all of it as much we can but that is a topic for another essay. Here, now, the topic at hand: a young man, preparing to enter what ought to be an exciting decade of his life, shackled by doubt, distrust and cynicism.

He is not wrong.

But every intuitive beat within me knows that he cannot be allowed to live there, in increasing despair for what is broken and seems unfixable. "The darkness around us is deep," (thank you for that piercing and honest line, William Stafford) and everyday evidence of its opposite is also true. How to certify this to a young man, or to any of us, in such a way that we do not feel misled or misheard? How do we live without naivete and yet also without the crushing weight of our failures to secure a hopeful future for the planet and all its inhabitants?

Six hours later, we carry what we can to the car. We discard the broken pieces of bookshelves in the dumpster two doors down and head out I90, driving west to the Berkshires. We have his clothes, books, guitar, music stands, posters of rap stars and perhaps 30 sweatshirts and a ridiculous number of baseball caps. I am at once proud of what I have helped him build and guilty about the excessiveness. No emotion feels singular these days; everything laced with an opposite. We sing as he plays guitar. He taught himself to play in the last three years, beginning with YouTube videos and over time finding folk who are farther along in the craft of songwriting to inspire him. Last year, for my 60th birthday, he wrote me a song, the refrain of which was that he would always be there for me. I believe him. We are steadied in each other's presence. He calls me "homebase." It is time for me to root him again at home, to a place of certainty where he can call out devastation *and* find it within himself to move forward anyway. To continue to play, sing, write, create, sweat in all those sweatshirts and build a life. It is what we owe the young ones in our lives...an honest path forward that includes the wholeness of living.

How do we live? This is really the question of our time, isn't it? How do we keep on doing this life thing when we know that so many of our choices cause harm or are simply not enough to mitigate the harm caused by generations of global ignorance and carelessness?

I know the elements of resilience, the pathways that activate perseverance: keep the body moving, eat well, sleep regularly, avoid toxins in your body, surround yourself with caring others, find time for joy, serenity, laughter, remember the meaning of your days, invest in that meaning, and hunt the good around you and within you. Actively, consciously, devotedly seek and savor evidence of goodness however and wherever it shows up. To this list, each element of which is substantiated by decades of research in mind/body medicine and resilience studies in psychology, I invite in the tonic of beauty.

In an interview with Krista Tippett[8] a few years before he passed, John O'Donohue said: "... there are individuals holding out on frontlines, holding the humane tissue alive in areas of ultimate barbarity, where things are visible that the human eye should never see. And they're able to sustain it, because there is, in them, some kind of sense of beauty...I love Pascal's phrase, that you should always keep something beautiful in your mind...if you can keep some kind of little contour that you can glimpse sideways at, now and again, you can endure great bleakness."

Dacher Keltner's[9] work on the impact of awe supports this understanding. Keltner suggests that experiences of awe, often evoked through participation in nature, can calm down our nervous system, quiet self-critical or anxious voices inside us, and enable a sense of connection to a larger world.

A kind of little contour of beauty that we can glimpse at ... it sounds like so little and yet I know that millions of people report that their suffering is eased as they find their way out into the forests and mountains, the streams and oceans, the prairies and the deserts, out into the beauty of the world around them.

As we arrive home and shuttle Jesse's stuff to his bedroom, I begin to think that we ought to take the time tomorrow to climb the hills of the land trusts near us—not to challenge our fitness, as we've done in the past, or to talk through the questions that haunt us, but to find, one more time, the tiny red eft that delighted him as a boy. Evident in the forests of the Northeast, they appear most often in the early morning hours, particularly when the ground is moist from rain. As a child he would pick them up from the walking trail, hold them in his hand for a bit, and carefully find a spot for them off the path that would keep them safer for a time. He'd talk to the little one, tell it a story of its family or of the woods, and place his hand on a patch of moss, or under a small pile of leaves under which the newt might hide. He let the newt climb off in its own time and would always say goodbye. For a few years—those years where there was no separation between wonder and the felt sense of forest and earth—he would ask to return, to find another little friend to greet, and care for, and carry on to a protected place. This was the effect of beauty for him—an elevation of amazement that came from the brilliant redness and the softness of the tummy and tickling of those four tiny toes in his palm.

I wonder if the curve of the newt's belly, now held in a palm large enough to hold the weight of guitars and dressers and broken shelves, will enable within him a bit more peace, enough to want to continue to find his place and a sustaining path forward, as hard as that might be.

Shimmers

"…beauty and grace are performed whether or not we will or sense them. The least we can do is try to be there."

—Annie Dillard

The least we can do…really…is to try to be present. Every single life on this planet, every cell-based organism, has an end date. And each convocation of eagles or shimmer of hummingbirds or exaltation of larks, exists as a unique entity in its own time. We are none of us the same. We are none of us irrelevant. And we are none of us eternal. The least we can do, truly, is to be present to the bounty in front of us, and if possible, if we are free enough within ourselves to be able to look for a moment beyond ourselves, to be both present and grateful.

I never mean, initially, to bring death into the conversation. I never sit down at the computer and say "Oh, I'll write about beauty and death, or hope and death, or wonder and dying." Still, it is always here as the great reality that colors everything. Hummingbirds are effervescent, in part, because they live merely 3-5 years. A jaguar in the wild may live 15 years. If lucky, the yellow Brimstone Butterfly, common in England and Wales, will live up to 13 months, by far the longest end date for these kaleidoscopic creatures. We all come with our finalities embedded and this, as much as anything, is what illuminates the beauty of any one thing: there is no promise that might halt inevitability. No escape at all. So, given this absolute fact, the least we can do is to try to be present to the specific beauties swooping and flitting their way past us. If nothing else, it is a kind of thank you.

A young man once dragged me from my cozy teacher's apartment on a Saturday night, leading me out to the Pacific Ocean off the coast of Cortes Island, about 250 kilometers north of Vancouver, British Columbia. He had been raving about the beauty of the ocean and I had held back, having a. no bathing suit and b. a middle-aged body and c. a dislike for freezing temperatures in August. It was the last night of our week-long retreat, and he wasn't having it—bullying me and the other participants, in the sweetest of ways, to wear whatever we wanted to wear but to get our butts in the ocean for a "moment" he claimed we wouldn't forget.

He worked unhappily for an oil company. His marriage was ending or had just ended and he had joined a group of much older women to study authenticity for a week. He didn't know he would be the only male, and he showed up fully each day anyway with a lively spirit. On that final night, I finally let go enough to say yes to him and met him after dinner, in the deep dark of evening. He led me to the ocean and as I inched my way in up to my knees, he had me swirl my hands to see the bioluminescent creatures about 8 inches below the surface, tiny beings the size of gnats. We played like this for a bit, contentedly, and had just decided to head back to shore when from across the bay, on the upper most ledge of a neighboring island, wolves begin to bay. A pack of them, facing north, were shadowed against the moon-full sky and the stars. Their sound, both prayerful and enlivening, locked us in place, which meant I was still there, on the beach, noticing the flickering illuminations of the sea, and tuned to the predators' call when the northern lights lit the sky behind the wolves, ribbons of yellow-green quivering through the blackness.

"Holy shit," were the first words that came to mind. And then, "Oh My God."

"After the one extravagant gesture of creation in the first place, the universe has continued to deal exclusively in extravagances, flinging intricacies and colossi down aeons of emptiness, heaping profusions on profligacies with ever-fresh vigor. The whole show has been on fire from the word go," wrote Dillard in *Pilgrim at Tinker Creek*, and in that moment, I felt the fire of her words, the fire of existence and the lightning strike of impossible beauty.

How is it possible that we have been gifted so much?

It does not matter whether you believe this planet was God-given or burst from a bang—no matter our origin, our Earth has been given so much loveliness. Just this morning on a regular walk through my regular town I saw two complete circular spider webs on parallel tree branches lit by the sun behind. Each web, about 12 inches across, glistened with morning dew and the light beam of the rising sun cast a gold tone to some of the strands. They seemed to have been placed deliberately to remind us of the closeness of near-perfection. I stood still, watching the light catch the dew and the subtle shift of the stands in the morning air, mesmerized by these works of art and struck by gratitude. Without striving or pleading, the morning had offered a natural gift—a vision that brought me closer to the sense that "thanks," as Anne Lamott tells us, is really one of the most essential prayers. And by prayer I don't mean a request for intervention but rather a devotion, an enthusiastic and deeply felt response to the call of the organic kingdom of the common spider and her creative offering, performed without audience or human-shaped agenda. That we find her forms beautiful is a bonus to us; that her creativity is driven predominantly by need—doesn't that somehow make it even more valuable? Even more worthy of our appreciation?

When someone gifts us a present there is often a reciprocity cycle built in: they give to us because we have given to them in the past; or because we can ensure their health or wellbeing; or because we are someone with whom they would like a closer future. Giving, or the potential for giving, has created a cycle of current and/or future continuous reciprocity. But these sudden surprises of webs or luminescence or the howling chorus of the wolf are without expectation. They are a grace, in the sense of the Old French word *gracier*, meaning favor or thanks, unbidden and untethered to our needs or wants.

That these gifts appear is a kindness in our living.

That we have nothing to do but be present to them is a generosity.

That we, in our attention, may experience uplift or awe or love or wonder or any of the other life-giving emotions is a bonus as vast as Kilimanjaro.

I think about that young man on Cortes Island now and then. It was easy for me and most of the women in our class to know that his moment of pain would not be the only story of his life. That after the divorce and the search for new work, sudden and surprising happiness would probably find its way to him.

He was young, with time on his side. He was open to learning, and so new information would continue to come his way to add to his wisdom. He had the capacity to see and to celebrate, and so the natural world would continue to be a balm to him and an encouragement. And he was young—did I mention that?—with so much yet to experience.

But despite our confidence in the possible futures ahead of him and our sureness that this very experience of pain had much to teach him that would aid him in impending choices, he wasn't so sure. He worried about the consequences of a job that was so debilitating and of a heart already scarred by a failed love. He wasn't certain he had the courage to rebuild along the lines of optimism I counseled. And he felt alone, unlike many in his town or his people. I don't remember what final words of wisdom I might have offered or that we, as a class, might have given. I do remember that we flooded him with appreciation for all he had brought the group and hugged the heck out of him on the last day.

Looking back, with an additional ten years or so under my belt, I wish I had the chance to offer him this thought: that his capacity to be present to the natural world was an opening to a wonder that might sustain him—if only he remained open. That even as people disappointed him, or as he was filled with doubt, the Earth itself was offering images that might imbue him with a kind of peace, and in that peace, he might find help or healing. Like those wolves howling against the sky, he truly was not alone in his cries—so many of us are so often wrestling with similar doubts while striving to grow.

Wherever he is now, I wish he could receive this care. I wish I could send missives of counsel and kindness through the ethers—that they might 'apparate' (a Harry Potter form of magical transportation) suddenly—that he might turn a corner on the way to work and a tree he passes every morning on his daily commute might unexpectedly host a web of love dedicated to him—a sparkle of unforeseen tenderness, brilliant in dew and light, carefully woven and resonant with the splendor that we two-legged ones can weave, made of kindheartedness, hopefulness and compassion.

SECTION TWO

Excellence

"If you want to build a ship, don't drum up the men to gather wood, divide the work, and give orders. Instead, teach them to yearn for the vast and endless sea."

—Antoine de Saint-Exupéry

The Giant

*"For in it may be seen most beautiful contours of legs,
with attachments of limbs and slender outlines of
flanks that are divine; nor has there ever been seen a
pose so easy, or any grace to equal that in this work...
in harmony, design, and excellence of artistry."*

—*Giorgio Vasari*

It is July 2022. Eight of us stand in silence, surrounded by
the hum of hundreds finding their way to the David, in
the Galleria dell'Accademia di Firenze, more commonly
known as The Accademia. We circle the statue for perhaps
twenty minutes, each of us finding an angle that captivates
our attention for a breath, until that curve leads the eye to
another aspect of a marble that seems impossibly true, nearly
alive. We have braved Florence in the heat of the summer,
for one day only, for one purpose: to stand in the presence
of Michelangelo's masterpiece. Five of us will return from
Florence the next day with Covid and we will all agree: our
experience of the virus does not matter at all in comparison
to the beauty of the northern Italian coastline and this one
moment in Florence in which we join generations of admirers,
awe-struck and changed by chiseled stone.

Excellence, from the Old French *"excellence"* and the Latin
"excellentia," refers to superiority, surpassing, loftiness, that in
which something or someone excels. It points to a rising above

the norm, an undeniable eminence—something both worth noting and unattainable by most. We speak of excellence in art, music, and performance, but also in thinking, in math modeling, in experimental design. It is a quality not bound to any one domain, and in its presence we are moved and often transformed. Sometimes we are changed in the specific desire to emulate—for example, to try sculpting stone in the ideal of Italy's greatest. Sometimes we are changed as we uncover a longing to strive for excellence in ways that are unique to us.

Leaving the Accademia, re-entering the piazza in the 92-degree heat of that day, I was not moved to register for an art class or read about sculpting. Rather, the desire that had become inflamed through witnessing this particular example of brilliance, was one of encouragement; I felt a motivating force as I mused, "If Michelangelo found mastery in his form, I might find mastery in the forms of my passions."

Excellence, like beauty, both inspires and motivates, and our attention to it may trigger within us a push and a bravery to become more than we have been, more even than we have thought possible.

Seeing the David had become a quest of mine ever since 2016, when I read a *New York Times*[10] article by Sam Anderson in which he reminds us that we like to believe that our greatest treasures are safe, beyond the reach, as he writes, "of the grimy world." In his piece he notes the history of threat centered in Florence: fanaticism, flood, earthquake, and politics all have had their sway at various times, causing harm to revered arti-facts. As just one example, he describes how, "In 1497, the fanatical monk Savonarola sent his followers door to door to gather the city's nonreligious art, books, clothing, musical instruments, then piled it all 50 feet high in the central square and set it on fire: the infamous Bonfire of the Vanities. (The spectacle was such a success that he repeated it the following year.)" The issue with the David isn't quite this, he continues, it is a fact of physical vulnerability. There are cracks in his ankles. Should the statue be tilted a mere 15 degrees, perhaps due to an earthquake or construction tremor, his ankles will not hold, and the David will fall.

This awareness of the statue's fragility brought a determined bent to what had been simply a wish in my life. After reading Anderson's piece, I had to figure out a way to get to Florence, because unlike the music of Mozart, which has been captured in so many forms (vinyl, digital, video and on paper) sculpture exists as a singular piece. If David falls, he cannot be known again in his entirety.

It took six years from that morning cup of tea with *The New York Times* to get myself to Florence, and that planning was worth every expenditure of my energy. No piece of art has ever struck me as fully or stayed with me as intensely as this.

When Anderson first saw David, he was 20 and the first word that came to his mind was "perfect." He writes: "'Perfect,' I know now, is not a terribly original response to the statue, nor a very precise one, but in that moment it filled my mind. It felt like a revolution—urgent, deep, vital, true.'" He was stunned and moved, fully attentive in a transformative sway. From there, after that initial touch of the perfect, he experienced what researchers know happens when excellence takes form and we are its witness: an alteration that breaks internal bonds.

"I stood there in my filthy Birkenstocks feeling a sense of religious transcendental soaring: the promise that my true self was not bound by the constraints of my childhood—by freeway exits, office parks, after-school programs, coin-operated laundry rooms at dingy apartment complexes...dead dogs, divorce...If such perfection could exist in the world, I felt, then so many other things were suddenly possible: to live a perfect life creating perfect things, to find an ideal way to be. What was the point of anything less?"

This is the gift of excellence. When we witness it, in forms that are meaningful to us, we may be transported. We may be changed.

Michelangelo was not the city fathers' first choice. Agostino di Duccio, the sculptor who had chosen the block of marble, soon to be nicknamed "The Giant" by the townspeople, compounded the natural deficiencies of the stone with his initial work and was fired. Da Vinci was considered, but he was known to have a profound distaste for sculpture. Others were consulted and rejected or rejected the task because of the marble's imperfections. The commission was finally given to 26-year-old Michelangelo Buonarroti. He began his work in 1501, more than 30 years after the Giant had been brought to Florence; it had sat for all that time, weathered by storm, assaulted by children and traffic and wind and shifting earth. To many, it seemed an impossible task to make anything of value, much less of beauty, out of this defective stone. Michelangelo toiled for more than two years, in a roofless shed built to protect his work, yet provide light, and when the initial statue was first revealed, the Vestry Board of the City determined it was already too beautiful to be placed up high in a cathedral, as had been their initial intent. It was decided to place the statue in the center of the city, in the Piazza della Signoria. It took 40 men more than four days to move the piece from the artist's shed to the plaza. There the David remained, still subjected to crowds, weather and tremors, until 1873, when the statue was moved indoors to the Galleria dell'Accademia, where he has been viewed by Sam Anderson and me, along with my seven companions and millions of others.

It is the effort, you see, that makes excellence extraordinary. Even if we have a natural gift, we must exert ourselves to create anything so far above the norm that it is worthy of reverence. We, the witnesses, know or sense that remarkable sweat and struggle from which excellence is achieved.

I am reminded of the words of soccer great Mia Hamm, "I am building a fire, and every day I train, I add more fuel. At just the right moment, I light the match."

We understand on some level that as we are inspired, we are also being challenged, a door opened to a question that can both expand and terrify us: Do we have it within us to persevere in our own way to achieve that level of mastery? Can we endure with tenacity and courage long enough to shape our talent or desire or chosen purpose from our own imperfect beginnings to a place of distinction and awe?

So few of us step through that door and prevail, in any field of endeavor. Yet each domain of our living has exemplars. Poetry, mathematics, architecture, dance, game design, philosophy, theater—in all fields, there is at least one human who has achieved greatness worthy of admiration and emulation, who has built the shed of their own work and toiled carefully enough to bring forward a David into our midst.

Positive Outliers

"After sleeping through a hundred million centuries we have finally opened our eyes on a sumptuous planet, sparkling with color, bountiful with life…Isn't it a noble, an enlightened way of spending our brief time in the sun, to work at understanding the universe and how we have come to wake up in it?"

—Richard Dawkins

I was once told a tale about an intervention program to reduce deviancy in young boys. Termed the Cambridge-Somerville Youth Study (CSYS), the multi-year program began in 1937 in Cambridge, Massachusetts with an initial cohort of 650 boys, ages 5-13, who had been termed pre-delinquent or average. Each boy was matched with a control group boy, who received none of the programming. The heart of the CSYS program, initiated by Richard Clarke Cabot (a professor of clinical medicine and social ethics at Harvard University) was "directed friendship," involving individual counseling through a range of activities and home visits. Counselors talked to the boys, took them on trips, tutored them in reading and math, helped them attend YMCA programs and summer camp, and encouraged church attendance. The boys in the treatment group received program support for an average of 5.5 years.

The program ended in 1945 and in a 30-year post-program evaluation, negative results were uncovered. For example, in her book *Crime and Family*[11] Joan McCord describes the poor results of this study in this manner: "Among the pairs in which the treatment family was uncooperative, the control and treatment boys were equally likely to turn out badly. Among the pairs in which the treatment family was cooperative, however, there were 27 pairs in which the treatment boys turned out better but 52 pairs in which the treatment boys turned out worse. These findings strongly suggest that the treatment itself had been harmful." Poor outcomes noted by analysts of the study included criminal activity, early death, and/or medical diagnosis as alcoholism, schizophrenia, or manic-depressive disorder.

McCord proposed that the failure of the program had to do with the uncooperativeness of some of the family environments; the withdrawal of support structures following the end of the study; poor relationships between some of the participants and their designated counselor; the lack of understanding about individual needs (what might work for one boy may make no sense at all for a different child); and failure to complete the program or to participate in all its facets. Though we may not fully understand what contributed to the negative results for so many of the boys, the study itself provided rich material for criminologists and social psychologists for many years.

And then in the early 21st century, positive psychology—the study of human thriving, wellness and growth—began to emerge, with a new direction and new questions for studying at-risk youth. Instead of only asking, "How might we help those who are failing?" positive psychologists might ask an additional question: "Who are the positive outliers—the children with all the concerning risk factors *who are succeeding despite those risks*—and what can we learn from them?"

In other words, if 2% of an at-risk middle school population demonstrate a capacity to succeed at work and in life despite their high-risk factors, what is it that are they doing? What do they know? What are their success factors and how might we apply those to the other 98% at risk? This attention to positive outliers changes the data field and our understandings. When we change the question, we change the conversation entirely.

In data sets, outliers represent data points that lie outside the norm of most of the other values in a data set. Positive outliers, sometimes termed positive deviants, represent individuals, teams, and communities who are outside the norm being studied—in a positive direction. The 1% of new sales hires who outperform others in an extraordinary manner. The 3% of artists, writers, dancers, musicians wrestling with illness who go on to perform at the top of their fields.

Or the families in a case study described by Save the Children,[12] looking at malnourishment in children in Northern Vietnam in the 1990's. The organization had a clear mandate to address the concern that 65% of children ages 1-4 living in North Vietnamese villages were malnourished. They wanted to find a sustainable, large-scale solution, based on local resources, which would have an impact within 6 months. Their approach was to look for the positive deviants: families who had found a way to nourish their children within the constraints of their village and were raising children who demonstrated no malnourishment. The NGO's staff discovered that within these outlier families, caregivers had been adding sustenance such as shrimp, crab, and fish to their children's meals. These elements were available to everyone but were generally deemed inappropriate for young children. Acting on this finding, the Save the Children staff developed activities with local communities to teach families about this simple change in diet, reducing malnourishment rates within months.

In any field of study, in any community or family system, positive outliers exist, representing the best of us. Excellence in behavior, thinking, adaption, and creativity is available to us for consideration and we might, as we find ourselves flooded with worry about the future, or despair at the sense of our own helplessness, find inspiration in attention to the positive outlier models living today. Not only do outliers inspire us with their accomplishment and the setting of a higher bar, they make it known that any beliefs we have about what is possible, are just that—beliefs. And beliefs can be changed.

In the field of climate change, this was recently made evident through the work of data scientist Hannah Ritchie. In her highly regarded TED talk, "Are We the Last Generation or the First Sustainable One?"[13] Ritchie changes the focus of the conversation about dystopic futures by sharing data representing dramatic positive shifts that are true, inviting us to change our perception of the role of today's younger generations. They might be the last generation of what has been eons of unconsciousness about global health, she suggests...or they might be the first to carry the banner of sustainability such that they become the ancestors of generations of climate care to follow.

As a speaker, writer, psychologist, I stand on the shoulders of those who have been the positive outliers in these fields. So many extraordinary voices, whose questions illuminated new ways of understanding. So much wisdom and lives worth emulating. Writing today, I cannot help but remember the flare in my belly when I first encountered the work of author Toni

Morrison, the first Black woman to win the Nobel Prize in Literature, in 1993.

Morrison's body of work and her profound presence in the field of literature as a fiction writer, essayist, editor, and professor, opened the door for new generations of female authors and of authors of color, demonstrating to us that narrative is not and never has been bound solely by the white, male Euro-centric perspective. In her Nobel acceptance speech, she reminded us that any use of language designed for the limitation of knowledge or representation must be rejected, as it does not create fertile ground for mutuality, respect, and the expansion of wisdom. She was, and still is, an exemplar of moral courage and excellence in her craft; reading her work early in my adulthood shook me to my core. Her stories, capturing an unflinching view of the injustice and the beauties of the Black American experience, were poetic, fearless, searing, honest and, in moments, soaring of spirit, and that is who I wanted to become. I wanted to become the kind of woman who used her voice generously and fiercely and authentically. The kind of woman who wasn't afraid to live into her passions boldly and who, without question, respected her own point of view.

In a dinner party hosted by Oprah Winfrey in 1996, Morrison expressed a turning point moment for her, when, burdened by the sense of many obligations, she took the time to write down the answer to the following question, "What is that, if I didn't do it, I would die?" And she had only two answers: mother her children and write books. Without those two, life wouldn't hold for her. And here, too, her excellence shone for me—an excellence in discernment, in knowing the right questions to ask, the questions that would infuse a life, not narrow it, or expand a capacity, not damage it. Because of her excellence, I was changed in my twenties, and she infuses me again with purpose today, nearly forty years later.

We may not have all the choices we could wish for in a lifetime. We may be raised in families with intense struggle, with limited resources and support, with histories of injustice and oppression that have made any kind of rising or health or school success a near impossibility. We may have believed the stories told us by others about what is impossible for us or who we cannot be. There are things we truly cannot control in our lifetimes. But no matter where we find ourselves, there are a few things we can often control: namely, our response to the stressors we face; and who we choose to emulate.

Seeking the positive outlier is more than an exercise in optimism or in statistical curiosity. It is a lifeline for any of us who wish to become larger than the restrictions placed on us or the categories through which we have been defined by others' perspectives. At various times in my life, I have moved forward because of the driving questions given me by the outliers who have touched me in meaningful ways, and I offer them to you now, as examples of how we might explore ourselves and our world, and as a thank you back to the extraordinary exemplars in my life.

Who am I in the presence of this?

What is it that, if you could not do it, life would not be worth living?

How big are you prepared to be?

What if the universe actually needed you exactly as you are?

How will you keep beauty and goodness alive in the part of the world that is yours to shape?

A Time of New Suns

"Everything is falling apart, but also, new things are possible...

We're in a time of new suns."

—*adrienne maree brown*

N adera* wears 10 bracelets of gold and beads on her left arm. Four rings grace her hand and her face is lined with wrinkles, which deepen when she smiles, which she often does this morning. I am working with Afghan refugee women through an American immigration center set up to receive high-achieving women brought to the US for safety in 2020 and 2021 when the Taliban had amped up their death threats against women leaders. When I first met Nadera, her smiles were far less frequent, with the trauma of her settlement here in a foreign land still so raw and fresh. Now, a year later, I see in her 70-year-old face a hint of lightness and hope, tinged with gratitude for the chance to meet again and share her wisdom. In the early weeks of resettlement, Nadera shared how she managed to get through the lonely, frightening days of linguistic isolation. Each morning, she told us, she made a cup of tea in her apartment, sat at the table by herself, and imagined an older, wiser Nadera across the table, listening to her talk about her challenges until she felt strong enough to enter the day.

*Nadera is the name I have chosen to protect her true identity.

"Everything we have been is falling apart," says author adrienne maree brown. "There is nothing new under the sun, but there are new suns." Nadera had been looking for new suns and in her imaginal conversations she began to find evidence of them. There is excellence, you see, in simply enduring.

We expect so much of ourselves. But post-trauma—post heartbreaking exile to a new land, when those you love are still at risk, when those you have worked for and with cannot work, cannot study, cannot build under a repressive regime and are so oppressed in every way, when those you leaned on for guidance and inspiration have been killed or jailed or beaten into silence, when the children of the future are afraid to go to school—we mustn't ask of ourselves brilliance or innovation or heroics, we must ask of ourselves only this: to survive long enough to see a new sun, and in that surviving to keep our lineages alive. Appreciation of excellence implies skill and achievement, but I have to suggest one excellence I have been moved by and expanded by over the course of my living: the extraordinary courage of daily survival across geographies.

Nadera loves being reminded that her practice has inspired others. I tell her that I have shared it in webinars and conversations around the world—that her example taught others in other lands, facing differing oppressions, how to enter a day in such a way that the balance of things has a chance to tilt toward growth or possibility or goodness. We know that resilience, hardiness, is sustained in this way: through daily actions that hold us steady and ignite even the tiniest bit of optimism. Nadera models for us an excellence that informs not only who we are, but who we might become, and who we must be if we are to endure.

If we search the roots of the word "excellence," there is no implication that it refers to the "mere" fact of survival—yet if we look at histories that have inspired humanity to continue to forge forward, they point toward the very importance of survival on its own terms. Perhaps this makes sense if we consider the thread of excellence that refers to merit, worth, value. Perhaps we ought to open the lens of our consideration of excellence so broadly that it can offer an appreciation of how a person might simply find a way through a time of horror. This feels particularly relevant now, as we witness a generation of young Americans at the highest risk of suicidality and debilitating anxiety and depression since WWII, and a level of mental illness heretofore unknown globally. Might a life-giving generosity to them, and to all of us really, be a dimming of attention on striving for excellence as achievement and rather a less glamorous, yet nonetheless effortful, choice to find ways to endure?

In the year following my first meeting with Nadera at a conference on resilience, I found myself emulating her choice. On cold winter mornings when the length of the day stretched grey and lonely, I would imagine an elder me, whitened by eight decades on the planet, wearing only comfortable fabrics, enjoying my Earl Grey with lemon, and reminding myself that all would pass, that no trouble lasts in the same form forever, that eventually a better idea would emerge through the whirlpool of doubt within me and that I was okay...not great...not wonderful...but okay. As I practiced her practice, I re-learned the value of enduring, of what Caroline Adams Miller calls "ordinary grit" in her book *Getting Grit*.[14] She describes this form of enduring in the evidence of "the unsung heroes who wake up every day and strive to succeed at goals that require persistence and dedication, but that also lack obvious external rewards or attention and acclaim from others. These men and women selflessly take care of disabled children while holding down full-time jobs, tirelessly advocate for the less fortunate as public defenders and social workers despite low pay and depressing outcomes or learn how to read in their sixties so that they can earn a long-desired high school degree." Or they persevere by moving through one day to the next, keeping their bodies alive, and each day attempting to discern how to be just a little bit more okay.

Nadia Murad comes to mind. Born in the village of Kocho, Iraq, one of many siblings. Her dream as a young girl was to become a hair stylist. Her family are Yazidis, a minority religious group targeted by ISIS. At the age of 19, in August of 2014, Islamic State fighters invaded her village, killing approximately 600 people, including her mother and many of her brothers and stepbrothers. She was taken prisoner and held captive, along with many other young women and girls. She was beaten, burned and raped repeatedly over a period of months, finally escaping one day when her captor left the house unlocked.

She had endured violence, rape, isolation. Then she endured re-entry in a world that knew little of her plight or her people. She not only kept her being alive, she kept alive the notion of her right for her people to exist, and through her activism, the rights of others to survive. By 2016 she had become a UN Goodwill Ambassador for the Dignity of Survivors of Human Trafficking and in 2018, she and Denis Mukwege, an African gynecologist, won the Nobel Prize for their efforts to end sexual violence as a weapon of war.

Enduring is often no small goal or process. It is the ground on which we enable the mosaic of our humanity to persist.

A parent caring day in and day out for a child with debilitating differences, often on the outside of the center of things. A young person surviving the horror of war dedicating their life to ending violence. An elder choosing to engage her mind each morning in a manner that cultivates strength and hope, so as to endure long enough to continue to contribute to the world. This is excellence in action. This is the best of us over time. This is who we are when pressed and who we must be if we wish this planet to remain our home.

We must become the new suns.

Courage, Tranquility, and Social Comparison

"It's an act of rebellion to be a whole person, right? It's an act of rebellion to show up as your whole self, and especially the parts that are complex, that are unfinished, that are vulnerable."

—*Courtney Martin*

It is July 2021. The Union of European Football Associations (UEFA) Cup tournament is being held at Wembley Stadium in England and for the first time in 50 years, England is in the championship match against Italy. In the first few minutes of the game, England scores and Italy struggles to find the goal for the remaining 43 minutes. Over and over they press, they dominate for long stretches, but with no result. At halftime, as the commentators discuss, Alessandro del Piero, the Italian analyst and former player, is asked what Italy must do to cap victory. Alessandro lowers his eyes for a millisecond, the tiniest of bows in recognition perhaps of the disappointment of those first 45 minutes, and then, his gaze now firm, he calls out the path. "Courage," he said, "and tranquility. They must return with courage and tranquility."

I can't imagine a more perfect response. To a game when we are a goal behind. To a championship upon which so much is at stake. To life itself. The courage to show up, take risks, and build toward a better future, along with tranquility, that calm inner state that rests in our certainty about who we are and what we have to offer.

If we have courage, our life expands. If we have an inner calm, our life stabilizes. Both hold value. Both are profoundly useful in the presence of excellence.

You see...there is a shadow side to excellence, to its presence in our lives. It triggers much that is positive—elevation, inspiration, motivation—and sometimes, because we are human and not always in possession of an inner peace, excellence may also trigger jealousy, embarrassment, even a feeling of guilt, of not being enough. And those feelings may lead to the opposite of growth: a shutting down, an internal cesspool of comparison to another; or a twisted attempt to somehow diminish the excellence of another, to explain it away or justify why we too have not offered as much or performed as well. Excellence may trigger the shadow side of humanity and it is in the creep of this shadow that we too must re-enter the game of living with courage and tranquility.

Negative social comparison is explained by social comparison theory, the theory that we evaluate ourselves based on our valuation of others, and where we stand relative to them. We judge ourselves relative to another's looks, material success, skill at task, level of achievement at work or contributions to society. Negative comparison means that we have judged ourselves inferior to others and have placed them, in our own internal Olympics of ranking, above ourselves.

Just after the pandemic, a new family moved into our county. The mother works in the school system, with children who need extra care. The father is a businessman and together they have adopted children and born a few, care for a variety of pets and foster some as well. Their home is always decorated for the seasons and their yard a playground of fun for the children. Within minutes of their presence in our circle, my guy and I said the exact same thing, "They are amazing. We suck."

And we are not wrong. In terms of pure hours of care for others above and beyond any work requirements, they win. We have fostered no one, nothing. They are better. We ought to be more like them.

Research has shown that those who experience frequent negative social comparison often feel envy and defensiveness, in addition to that sucky feeling of not being good enough, and are likely to engage in behaviors such as lying to feel better, blaming others to make them feel worse, and a general, chronic unhappiness. They tend to exhibit more destructive behaviors. Just think of the child you knew who could not tolerate anyone else winning the game and would upend the board or quit the race midway so that no one else could win. Or the political aspirant who falsifies their past in order to win against a more decorated opponent. Or the culture that makes fun of other cultures. The North is better than the South. Country folk are more real than city folk. Our town is better than your town.

As social creatures, we want to belong, and we often need to belong in such a way that we feel like we are better than others. Not only is this destructive to our relationships, triggering bias and bullying if not outright violence, it ruins any opportunity to become larger within oneself, to become more like those whom you admire, trapping us in a cycle of low self-regard and its consequent sufferings.

It is here, as we watch others on social media have "their best lives" or meet others on the street who give more or watch others on stage win the award we covet, that we must find our way back to root in Alessandro's suggestion: courage and tranquility.

For there is another option: upward social comparison—comparing ourselves to others who we deem as better and using that comparison as a source of inspiration and energy.

Instead of upending the game board, we might say, "If she can do this, I can too." "If he can build that, I wonder what I might build?" "If they have found a way to rescue a species, how might I save another?"

In October 2024 I witnessed Dr. Tererai Trent of Zimbabwe captivate an audience of women leaders in business with her story of emerging from a system in which education is withheld from girls, a system embedded in poverty, patriarchy, and oppression. In her 40-minute talk she enthralled her audience with her courage, her determination to find a way to become educated, and once educated, to give back. As just one small example, when she was in her early 20s and the mother of five children, she and her mother had to work six months to raise $20 so that she could take two high school courses. And the first few times she took those first few courses, she failed. It took her 8 years to get her high school degree, while also farming and raising small children, learning by sunlight, lanternlight or candlelight. Despite the stressors, she persevered and kept her dream alive, eventually earning a college degree and then her doctorate in plant pathology. Today she leads a global foundation, the Tererai Trent Foundation, to sustain empowered rural communities where all children have access to quality education, supported by socially engaged business models. Since her foundation's establishment in 2011, 40,000 children have been educated, 51% of them girls.

Her mantra in those long days of mothering and studying and doing all she could to keep her dream alive? "It is achievable."

We, the audience, leapt to our feet the second she finished her speech. Many of us had tears in our eyes; we were stunned. For a moment, in the glow of her achievement and her rampant generosity, I know that most of us felt elevated and inspired. We felt that our dreams would be achievable too. Of course they would be! We had been scented with her aura! Imbued with her energy and her blessing! Transformed by her goodness!

And then...walking back to our rooms...imagining our lives on paper next to hers...I know that some of us felt less than. I heard the familiar refrain in my own head as her excellence swirled about me, "She's amazing. I am not. I've had every privilege a white, educated, middle class woman in a free country could possibly have and I have not built one well, one school, patched one home, or freed one child."

This is accurate.

And yet...and yet...I cannot be Tererai. It is an unfair ask... not because I couldn't build a foundation and work for the things she found meaningful...not because any of us couldn't. It is unfair because it is too limited an ask. Too small a doorway to walk through.

I could try to imitate her life...that is one way to leverage a story of excellence, so that more excellence is made possible in the arena she chose. Or I could hold a larger ask, cross a wider threshold: how can I allow her story to inspire the goodness that is mine to offer? How might I step into the values she offers and have them illuminate mine and translate the resonance of the two into the tasks that are mine to take on, on behalf of the land I am here to steward, the people I am here to influence? How might I meet her in the field of generosity and hard work and resilience and connection with my own lantern?

It would not be a bad thing to be just like her. And there are many who are enlivened by work of education, business and community building in rural areas. It would, in fact, be a wonderful thing to have a second Tererai in the world...but it is not my thing. And let me be clear...by my thing, I do not mean it is not a personal interest of mine and so I shouldn't have to take it on, in the way a teenager might not want to sign up for the school play, because it isn't her thing. What I mean by "my thing" is that it is not the channel of goodness that is unique to me. It is not where my deepest energies race or highest values soar. It is not where the best of me intersects with the needs of the world.

Dance exemplar, innovator and instructor Martha Graham said it this way, "There is a vitality, a life force, a quickening that is translated through you into action, and there is only one of you in all time, this expression is unique, and if you block it, it will never exist through any other medium; and be lost. The world will not have it. It is not your business to determine how good it is, not how it compares with other expressions. It is your business to keep it yours clearly and directly, to keep the channel open."

Here is a question perhaps worth living into then: How might I enable the excellence and moral goodness of a Tererai Trent to influence the quickening force within me such that I am raised and because of that raising, my offering to the world is brought to a new level of contribution?

～

We are back, then, to courage and tranquility.

Could I be tranquil enough in myself to be at peace with the channel of my one, individual, specific offering? Could I respect my expression, to borrow from Graham, and be courageous enough to expand at the same time?

If I am able to do so, my living becomes a part of the lineage of Dr. Trent.

I become one radiating aspect of the legacy she brings to our world; an aspect perhaps far removed from the building of a classroom for 5-year-old girls in Zimbabwe, but an aspect of her lineage, nonetheless.

In this way, goodness thrives and swells.

In this way, excellence becomes manifest in a multiplicity of forms, all needed, all vital.

The Galvanizing Upward
Spiral of Excellence

*"By appreciation, we make excellence in
others our own property."*

—Voltaire

In Jacques Lusseyran's stunning autobiography, *And There
Was Light*,[15] he recalls the moment as a young boy, recently
blinded, when he experiences an epiphany of gratitude. With
the loss of his sight, much was adjusted and in the internal
re-wiring of neurons and senses, his hearing improves to the
point of astonishment. He writes:

> *"I needed to hear and hear again. I multiplied sounds to
> my heart's content. I rang bells. I touched walls with my
> fingers, explored the resonance of doors, furniture and trunks
> of trees…with sound I never came to an end, for this was
> another kind of infinity."*

Another kind of infinity.

Lusseryan grows up to be the kind of man who uses his gifts
for the betterment of humanity. Alarmed as a teenager at the
rising tide of Nazism, he decided to learn German in order to
listen to German radio broadcasts. This was but one of many
skills he used as a founder of a resistance group in Paris at
the age of 17. For two years he recruited resistance fighters,
spread the news of German plans, warned French citizens, and
did what he could to protect his people. Eventually he was

captured, betrayed by a colleague, and sent to Buchenwald concentration camp. He survived the war, and after a time moved to America, where he became a university professor of French Literature and Drama at Middlebury College in Vermont, among other colleges.

In a *Bennington Banner* newspaper article, dated July 20, 1964, he is quoted as saying, "Blindness does not bring about the kind of invalidism one might expect. Not only are there compensations, but an entirely new world is opened up in sensations and perceptions…the latent powers in man are really enormous."

Lusseyran, a successful and sought-after professor, is most noted for his character in the many articles written about him: his humility, his pride in his students, his desire for education to become a place of excellence, and his love of life.

Decades later, Anthony Doerr, an American novelist from Boise, Idaho, acknowledges a debt of gratitude to Lusseyran in his novel, *All the Light We Cannot See*.[16] He writes, "He (Lusseyran) lost his sight at a young age…What's beautiful about it is that his parents didn't see it as a disability; he never gave in to despair. He led a busy boyish life, and he became convinced, in an almost mystical way, that the world is composed of light and that he figured out some ways to actually see it." Doerr's novel, centered on the light we cannot see, essentially radio waves, and also the light of knowledge, kindness, and love, won a Pulitzer Prize in 2014. In speaking further about his debt to the Frenchman, Doerr honors Lusseyran's ability to know, as a member of the resistance, whether a new recruit would be trustworthy or not, just by hearing the recruit's tone of voice and feeling his presence.

Without sight, Jacques found a way to see.

His capacities, his endurance, his devotion to literature, his fight for humanity—each of these contributed to the inner and outer excellence that pushed Doerr to devote ten years to a novel that might honor this man.

This is why we must seek excellence.

This is why, especially in the harshest moments of injustice, violence, betrayal, and oppression, we must look for the exemplars—those who in both ordinary and extraordinary ways elevate what is possible.

Excellence inspires. It pushes us to grow, to try, to question what might yet be true.

And in our gratitude, the heartfelt appreciation of the excellence of others, we give ourselves a chance to become larger within: to move out of any narrow point of view that is centered only on ourselves, to consider how we might bring forward that which we admire in others.

Biological lineages are what they are. We each are born into certain genetic strains, cultural and geographical determinants, and nationalities. We, in our younger years, have layered expectations of race, gender and preference onto the norms of our local communities and religions. But as we age, choice emerges. The choice to choose other lineages to which we feel we might belong. The lineages of sculptors or musicians. Of scientists or educators. Of physicians or pie makers or, in my case, the lineage of those who believe that words matter: the poets, essayists, orators and novelists. We have the chance to choose who informs our perspectives and actions. We are free, no matter our circumstances, to learn from the myriad options of being human, and be stirred and encouraged by those who make sense to us in ways that have nothing to do with our biological or childhood inheritances.

Moral excellence is not bounded by any tribe. Nor is the excellence of achievement. It has emerged throughout history in the form of every gender, every nationality, every people. As Lusseyran himself said, "Our fate is shaped from within ourselves outward, never from without inward."

And while that may not be fully true—just consider the fates of those oppressed, impoverished, marginalized, born into war—what is true is that we can affect some aspects of our living by lifting our heads, opening our minds and hearts and considering who we might want to model ourselves after.

To whose excellence might we link in our adulthood?

Ada Limón[17] is our first female United States Poet Laureate of Mexican and Latino heritage. She is known for her intimacy, emotional resonance and appreciation of natural and animal kin. On my desk is this excerpt from her poem "How to Triumph Like a Girl":

> I like the lady horses best,
> how they make it all look easy...
> I like their lady horse swagger,
> after winning...
> But mainly, let's be honest, I like
> that they're ladies ...

Don't you want to lift my shirt and see

the huge beating genius machine

that thinks, no, it knows,

it's going to come in first.

On my desk next to Limón is a stanza from our first National Youth Poet Laureate, Amanda Gorman, a woman of color, who, at the age of 23, astounded the world when she read her poem, "The Hill We Climb" at the 2021 inauguration of President Joe Biden. Her words:

So let us leave behind a country better than the one we were left…we will rebuild, reconcile and recover in every known nook of our nation…for there is always light if only we are brave enough to see it, if only we are brave enough to be it.

And on my bedside table, next to the candles and the Chapstick, next to the pile of books I have begun, and the cards I cannot bear to throw away, is a handwritten note, words I have copied from Dr. Robin Wall Kimmerer, Native American botanist, author, professor, and environmentalist, found in her seminal work, *Braiding Sweetgrass*.[18] Her words articulate the commitment of indigenous peoples to honor each other and the land and all that the land provides in order to ensure the wellbeing of all species:

Know the ways of the ones who take care of you, so that you may take care of them…Take only what you need. Take only what is given. Never take more than half. Leave some for others. Give thanks for what you have been given…Sustain the ones who sustain you and the earth will last forever."

It is unlikely that in my lifetime I will win a Pulitzer, become a world-renowned environmental activist or an honored professor. I won't rescue hundreds from invading Nazis and I won't ever be the youngest to win anything on a national stage.

And still…I have adopted myself into the lineage of these women. I sit in my bedroom in a small town in a quiet county in the northeast of the United States and although my geography might be small, my genetic inheritance common, my age a bit past due, still I can bring a glimmer of their goodness, their potency, their care alive. I can feel the beat of the horse-heart within me and stand steady in the flow of generosity of the land and all its beings and like these word-bringers be brave… oh let me be brave…and seek the light and see the light and beam the light.

What is your prayer, my friends?

Moral Beauty
(Goodness)

"The mycorrhizae may form fungal bridges between individual trees, so that all the trees in a forest are connected...They weave a web of reciprocity, of giving and taking. In this way, the trees all act as one because the fungi have connected them. Through unity, survival. All flourishing is mutual."

—Robin Wall Kimmerer

The Generous Exchange

*Those who contemplate the beauty of the earth find
reserves of strength that will endure as long as life
lasts. There is symbolic as well as actual beauty in
the migration of the birds, the ebb and flow of the
tides, the folded bud ready for the spring. There is
something infinitely healing in the repeated refrains
of nature—the assurance that dawn comes after
night and spring after the winter.*

—*Rachel Carson*

This is the world I want to dwell in. This is the place I want
to keep my attention fixed upon—the place where the
sun assuredly rises and the peonies of summer return, despite
the cold freezes and warm breezes of our climate-disrupted
winter. Here, in the world Carson depicts, is where I want to
fully live: where nature continues to sooth and fascinate and
where we, as stewards of the earth, are invited, through those
constant yet flowing rhythms of migration and budding, to be
repaired and healed and moved.

Rachel Carson, a marine biologist and environmentalist,
was one of the first voices to call out the devastation we wreak
upon the world in her seminal work *Silent Spring*,[19] published
in 1962. It is she who was also more prepared than many to
understand the significance of the template of our living—this
gorgeous planet where so much is available to us to learn from

and to heal with. Through her science she found much to be enthralled by. Through her care, we found much to be motivated to care for in return.

This morning, aware that I was a toddler when *Silent Spring* and other early voices of the nascent environmental movement found their way to bookshelves, I return to the patch of earth granted me to guard, a small patch of Western Massachusetts with the rising hills of the Berkshire Mountains behind.

Four Adirondack chairs encircle the stone fire pit behind my house, facing southeast where the sun rises in the morning and the sky is largest at night. If I sit exactly right, I can pretend there is little between me and the creatures of October Mountain, with whom we share a gentle pact: black bear, white-tailed deer, coyote, red fox, bobcat, the occasional mountain lion, and fisher cat. Red-tailed and Cooper's hawks cross through our backyard as often as the students who have laid a trail between their houses and the high school nestled below the slope of our lawn.

Behind the high school is the mountain, and on that mountain life teems. Nearly every day I sight a child or a creature, crossing our yard to the school and home again, or searching the backyard grounds for ferns, berries, nuts and grasses, and then returning to a bed hidden under the mountain pines. Their travels are common, regular, frequent, and no less precious, for in the intersection of their walking an enchanting coherence happens.

Here I sit this morning, tea in hand, a velour blanket on my lap, watching two middle-school boys, with backpacks, baseball caps and one with a cell phone, cross the edge of our yard, enter the trail to the south, and head through the high school's upper soccer field to the side door of the building below. They speak to each other closely, and I have no idea, despite my best spying ears, what they discuss. X-box? Exams? Friends? Lunch? It could be anything and nothing of import at all but more important to me is to notice that they pass not four feet from a small deer, frozen against the brown grasses of October. They don't see her. Don't comment on her tender beauty, the way her head is still, alert, with only a twitching ear to indicate her aliveness. Her tail is steady. Her feet rooted. Yet emanating from her, as clear as day to me from my perch on the hillside, is the vibrant concussion of energy between her urge to flee and the demand to freeze. She is listening with every fiber of her being, radiating alarm, as the boys reach the apex of the yard and turn toward the school.

With three more steps they bend away, and I expect to see the deer run, leaping away—but she doesn't. The boys reach the edge of our land, turn south toward the school, their foot-falls softer now, their voices disappearing, and she relaxes in place, as a yogi might, and settles into her pose. Tension falls off her like a blanket and she reaches for a leaf, just at fore-head height, nibbles the edge and chews. No need to process the fright, call a therapist, or journal through the night. One moment she is alert and on edge, the next she is at peace.

And in her peacefulness, I am made glad. Literally remade in the moment, laced with gladness.

"Things come together and fall apart," wrote Pema Chrodron.

"Dawn comes after night and spring after winter," said Rachel Carson.

And she, the fawn of this day, states the same: difficult moments arise and then fall. All is in motion, and no moment is final. Larger rhythms are at play here, within us and around us, and if we simply choose to attend with an open mind, we too might find a way to allow a moment to be, and then allow it to pass.

Something cohered in our morning moment together.

An integration of diverse elements—two boys, a small brown being, and a witness. Our bodies formed a triangle for a brief period and in the geometry of our connection, life's way affirmed itself. Without the boys, she would not have been stilled. Without her fright, I would not have seen the release of that fright; I would not have been reminded again of the "infinite healing in the refrains of nature." Would it have happened without my presence? Yes. Does it matter? Not so much. Life presents itself to us for our learning in every moment wherever we are.

"Suffering," I once wrote, "may not end but it will change in tone and texture and the good will come again." Moments come and go. Even pain is not separate from the inherent rhythmic shifts of our living.

Seeing this evidenced again so simply this morning, so perfectly quietly, brought to me a delight and a determination to hold fast here. To dwell in the beauties and mysteries Carson saw and honor them for all they bring to us.

I can be the deer. We can be the deer—alert and triggered and fearful and then at peace. We too are of the natural world. We too are in its exchange.

A second consideration. In writing about the nature of gifts, as in the gifts of the world to us, Robin Wall Kimmerer writes in *Braiding Sweetgrass*: "(This) is the fundamental nature of gifts: they move, and their value increases with their passage. The fields made a gift of berries to us, and we made a gift of them to our father. The more something is shared, the greater its value becomes."

Can we not then consider the moments of our witnessing

to be a part of this gift-giving economy, an additional rise and fall of knowledge layered upon the cadences of the natural kingdoms? Can we not shape our witnessing to fit this frame? The deer and the boys—it all would have happened without me, but in my seeing, really seeing, the pattern of rising and falling on an ordinary morning, I am gifted knowledge and in return may pass that gift forward here, participating now in a concurrent rhythm. As moments rise and fall, they present themselves to us to understand and learn from, and to share that knowledge just as the deer shared her nature, just as the strawberries Kimmerer refers to offered theirs.

Here is where the roots of moral goodness rest: in our awakened awareness that we are not isolated. How we live—what we choose to bring, to offer, to honor—matters. Our lives are connected to the grand natural kingdoms and to each other. When we see ourselves as interrelated, interwoven, it is much harder to cause harm. Then we begin to understand that our patch of ground, our square of living, is not simply ours to inhabit, but ours to tend, so that others may experience the benefit of our tending, and we may participate as fully as possible in the grand exchange of generosity, of beneficence.

On September 30, 1207, Jalal A-din Mohammad Rumi was born in Persia. He lived and died more 6,260 miles from my backyard fire pit. He devoted his life to justice, poetry, scholarship, and faith and became one of the most influential voices not only of his land and of his spiritual faith, but of his time.

His voice echoes throughout texts and treaties of seekers to this day and his works are quoted across all borders of our world in the halls of temples, the shelves of bookstores and in cards handwritten by our friends to remind us that we are not alone.

I am not in any way related to Rumi. I don't believe I had a magical incarnation with him back in the day and there is little evidence of his determined passion for Sufism in my living. Yet I have been guided for decades by the gift of his faith in humanity, his call to inner peace and his brave, impassioned longing for connection to the divine.

When my friend Etta passed, I read his words at her service: "Out beyond ideas of wrongdoing and right doing there is a field. I will meet you there." When my brother died, I put together a small altar in my home, in homage to all he had brought us, and centered underneath a six-inch ceramic red heart, lay the quote: "What you seek is seeking you." And all that I do in my resilience teachings, my positive psychology guidance and my daily explorations of healing and growth rest in Rumi's wisdom: "The wound is the place where the Light enters you."

Rumi's grave in Konya, where he was buried next to his father, is one of the most visited pilgrimage sites in the world. His tomb is inscribed with these words: "When we are dead, seek not our tomb in the earth, but find it in the hearts of men." This seems to me to be the most generous exchange of all—the understanding that our lives may continue on in the hearts of others. His wisdom is as alive to me as the deer and the boys walking through my yard. It is a gift across centuries that informs my capacity to stay still and notice, to see the treasure hidden in such small moments, and to take the risk of sharing what I have seen in my own small way.

Such is the unstinting flow of exchange available to all of us.

These are the strawberries of my days—a sweetness and an offering evidenced in a particular season and a particular land so long ago and so far away from my American hills, but no less potent for its distance in time or geography. I have received from Rumi. I choose to extend his wisdom forward.

This is what I can offer.

This is how I participate in the natural cycles to which Carson and Kimmerer bear witness: the land gifts its fruits, the animals their organic natures, humans their wisdom... none of it separate...all existing in a replenishing flow that we can enter in our own way at any time. And it is in this flow that we find the rising of goodness, the rising of the best of ourselves: our generous, attentive, hearts.

Heart

"In the end, only kindness matters."

—Jewel

The two times my daughter, Raphaela, stopped and opened her car to pick up a unhoused man and bring him to a store—once for a phone, once for clothing and food—I did not respond well. Meaning, when she called me those evenings, long after she had returned her companion(s) to their spots, her throat thickened with elation, I heard nothing at first of the wonder such an act illuminated in her, thought nothing of the kindness radiating through her 110-pound frame, considered little of the possible repair of one vein of an exiled heart; instead, I reacted the way you might imagine a panther parent might react—kind of viciously. Despite years of modeling care for others, teaching both my children to give, to look for the marginalized and pay attention and offer what one can, I felt only fear, and my fear sounded an awful lot like rage and the crazed terror of a threatened animal.

Fair enough, you might say, you only wanted her safe. She is yours, and you wanted to protect her, warn her of the dangers of larger, strange men. And you would be right; I was right. And I was also wrong for, though she is mine in a biological, familial, perhaps even karmic sense, she is also "hers" and of the world. She is both mine and far more than that implies. She is a singular representation of humanity, as were those she sheltered, and as such has a place and a path that can only be known through the experimentation of life that is hers to make. This really isn't a note about authentic paths or destiny even, it is about excellence and how sometimes we can't see it, or aren't capable of seeing it because we are too constricted by dread. I dread that such an act may steal her from me and I panic about living without her. Still, this is exactly how I raised her. To host a heart large enough to look—to truly see—to care, to act.

Goodness toward others is one of humanity's highest virtues. Captured as moral excellence in the field of psychology it is understood to be essential to the survival of our species and essential also to living a life of meaning and value. In this same field of study, moral excellence is also seen as a form of beauty—the beauty of the inner essence of humanity. It is a transcendent quality of our humanness, moving us beyond the self-centered concern for personal survival and wellbeing into the larger realms of kinship. As we care for each other, as we are kind and thoughtful and active in that thoughtfulness, we ensure survival both literally and spiritually and we are brought to the best of ourselves. We embody excellence.

If we are to become better as a species, we are sometimes required, even when it is terrifying, to move alone, beyond protection, toward this excellence, this beauty. In her actions, Raphaela became the best of us. Me, in my initial reaction, not so much.

⌁

There is a photograph, buried in a box in the basement, of me at the age of 23. I was newly married, and my spouse, an expert skier, brought us to vacation in St. Moritz, Switzerland.

I had never skied before, and after I took a few beginner lessons I decided (as those lessons were not fun but incredibly awkward and cold) to take a risk and do something else. I had seen people hang gliding down the mountain range and signed myself up for an afternoon session. In the photograph of my virgin descent, you see me buckled in and strapped onto the actual glide expert in front of me, his hands steering us in ever widening circles as we ride thermals down into the valley. I have been instructed to simply sit back in the strap-made seat, relax and enjoy the ride down, but I cannot. The sun radiates so violently off the fresh snow that our sunglasses are of little use. We are surrounded by luminosity, a crystalline shine, and the wind loops around and under us in giant circular waves. I am caught in spirals of uplift and turn and feel as an eagle might, both carried and emboldened by larger forces. I am thrilled in every cell in my body—alive, awake, astonished—and I cannot just sit back. There is no part of me prepared to sit back. "I sing the body electric," wrote Whitman and in that ride I become vibrant with the thrum of energy encircling me. In the photo, I hold onto the back of the guide and my body is perfectly straight. I am an exclamation of elation and freedom. I am ecstatically free.

The two times my daughter stopped and opened her car to pick up someone unhoused and care for them, in the specific ways they needed care in those exact moments, she too felt free. The joy in her voice could not be contained. Her life, her way, mattered. She felt significant and engaged in acts of meaning so tied to her sense of self that she too, had been electrified and embraced by life itself. Excellence here has nothing to do with accomplishment but of the moral clarity of seeing one's place in life as a conduit of goodness—of choosing to see and act on behalf of others. For some of us, this is where and how we feel most alive, connected to the larger ineffable forces which ensure that we are part of the interdependent flow, a flow that necessarily must include all races, identities, geographies, circumstances of living.

In the joy of my spiraling ride over the mountain I experienced the vibrancy of my own life force, a vibrancy existent only to me and for me. In my daughter's joy, she joined lineages of peoples throughout time whose central attention is the lifting of others and through that care of the stranger, experience a lifting of self as well. Moral excellence, by its very nature, is beyond the self. It has no regard, to quote British social theorist Harriet Martineau, for classes and professions. It is generous to the benefactor as well as to the recipients for it centers the heart far beyond itself and as it does so it triggers a consequent positive effect. As we witness moral beauty in others, we become elevated and inspired to action; we become kinder in response and more likely to care for others. We find ourselves wanting to be like these exemplars, and not only do we feel better about ourselves and life, but certain tendencies are also catalyzed deep within our psyche that literally change how we behave.

Raphaela helps a man and shares her tale; I am more likely to donate to a food pantry or volunteer at a school because of having witnessed her beneficence. Even the sharing of this story—here, now, years later—may inspire positive action in others. Think of how often one story of generosity between others has been at the root of your own movement toward another. How one example from within your own family or community tree has initiated circles of care. It is how we become more alive…and how we ensure the continuation of life itself.

The unhoused in our town have increased in number. Each day as I travel ordinary roads I see evidence of poverty, of loss, of tenuous holds on survival. My friends and I exchange stories of what we know: which one has a child, which one can be found panhandling at the Marshalls/CVS plaza, who stands at the nearby bookstore entrance. We talk about going to the bank and withdrawing so we have enough small bills to donate and how many of us upped our donations as the holidays drew near. We worry about the impending storms and read the local paper to find out if a new shelter facility will, in fact, be built. We are honest about the guilt of our privilege, admiring of the few among us who are on top of the volunteer moments available to serve at the dinners organized by local churches and temples. We are, in general, decent people, but not once have I or any of my peers put an unhoused person in our cars, listened carefully to what they needed, and brought them exactly that. I do not know what differentiates my daughter from myself or others, what constellation of genes and personality and strengths enables within her a larger courage. As her mother, I do not want her to do this again, at least without a national guardsperson in the car with her. But as a woman, I long to understand how she comes to be so compelled and how I too, might be more like her.

Rainbows

"Try to be a rainbow in someone else's cloud."

—*Maya Angelou*

Last night I watched a haunting, inspiring documentary, "Four Winters," featuring seven Jewish partisans who survived WWII hiding in the forests of Poland, fighting each day for survival while doing all they could to halt the Nazi genocide. The film's narrators, women and men who each found their way to the woods as teens or young adults, talk of the horrors, despair and starvation in their forest campgrounds and, in the way of all humanity, find a way to share the moments as well that remind us of our magnificence.

In one tender moment, one of the men recalls raiding a farm for food, returning with a few pigs to feed the group... and then pauses to say, "and one of the women was kosher—so we took a chicken too." In the presence of starvation, we might imagine that kosher dietary laws take a far second priority—fair enough—but what he showed us, this teenager turned freedom fighter, is that even with death hovering like a velociraptor at every corner, it is possible to care for another, one chicken at a time.

It is not difficult to be a rainbow in the cloud of a day no matter where we are or the circumstances of that cloud. We simply have to want to be. We must have the desire to do so, the time to do so and the mental creativity that enables that desire. Collecting the bigger stories of our magnificence has been a passion of mine since childhood but I've also spent that same lifetime noting the small generosities; ones that appear just as rainbow does—suddenly, briefly, ephemerally.

Once a woman handed me her baby, an infant no more than four months old, the week after the loss of my brother. I had returned home to be with my children and begin the long hard work of grieving and she, the rabbi's wife, came over with her babe in arms, sat near me on the couch and said, "I thought it might help to feel life," and let me hold her baby as he rested. I don't know how she knew to do this, nor what vulnerability she had to quell to allow someone distraught to hold something that precious, but she was right. It did help— not in any way I could name, but for those few moments, while her infant slept on my lap, I wasn't despairing or fighting hard not to despair. He calmed me and that was a grace.

During that same time, without ceremony, an old friend dropped off the best butter pound cake my family has ever eaten. Butter, sugar, flour, eggs. So simple and so consequential. She left a three-word note with the cake, "Butter always helps." And she was not wrong. We hadn't spent time together in perhaps seven years but her traverse across the borders of our town, to find me and gift me in the heaviest of moments dappled the day with color. I imagine the same for the woman in the forest—hearing the raiding party return, watching the bonfire built to roast the pigs, and then the sudden drop of a squawking chicken at her feet—and an arc of color cascading into her heart.

In Sonja Lyubormirsky's esteemed work, *The How of Happiness*,[20] she writes that the practice of gratitude has at least eight benefits, one of which is that it elevates or encourages moral behavior. The behavior she refers to is generosity, the quality of being kind, magnanimous. As we are grateful to others, we are generous in spirit. As others witness our appreciation, they are more likely to be kind to another, or to themselves. These two elements, appreciation and generosity, entwine together like the two strands of our DNA molecules. They are linked by the virtue we call "love of humanity," and truly represent the best of us. The larger stories I share here of moral goodness or extraordinary beauty are compelling and inspiring but there is a significant place in our living as well for these small glimmers of the rainbow we might choose to bring forward. These tinier gestures, the cakes and flowers and thoughtful moments of presence, often give us a reason to keep on keeping on—in other words, to choose to live. And in a world rife with depression, suicidality and anxiety, this is not a bad thing at all.

Love of humanity, classified as one of the six virtues of human beings by positive psychology researchers at the VIA Character Institute, refers to the qualities of love, kindness, generosity, and social intelligence. The common thread among these elements is a conscious, altruistic care for others, through which we find the hope to face what must be faced and the will to contribute to the cycle of care ourselves. We are not just inspired to get out of bed, but to do so in a way that benefits others. That butter cake continues to live in my heart, and I have replicated my friend's gesture of offering that cake time and time again.

We are fascinated, too, by the evidence of this care in other species, and especially across species. The cow adopting the injured duckling. The dog agreeing to nurse six abandoned kittens. The horse becoming best friends with the goat and appearing to mourn when the goat dies. We are astonished by this emotive largesse, and I think a bit humbled—if a Great Dane, Kate, and a fawn, Pippin, can learn to care for each other, why we might wonder, is it so tricky to be kind to that neighbor down the street who seems a bit different? If you spend any time, as I do, seeking videos of these benevolent relationships, eventually you realize that care is bound by only by man-made rules. We are meant to reach out toward the other; it is only our fear of the other that suppresses what appears to be an encoded instruction to tend and befriend one another. Pippin the fawn had been injured, and when Kate's owner brought her into their home to recover, Kate— of a species known to hunt deer—snuggled up to Pippen and let her lie in her dog bed. And even as Pippen became well and returned to the forest, she would come back to Kate's yard periodically for a romp and a cuddle, just as friends do.

Social psychology research affirms this tendency to care in humans. Empirical evidence has shown that infants as young as eight months are willing to share toys, and at 14 months of age will help an adult experimenter finish a task. As they age into school years, children show that they are willing to voluntarily share resources. Health psychologist Kelly McGonigal, in her best-selling work *The Upside of Stress*,[21] reminds us that the tend-and-befriend response is not just a response to stress but a health-driven mandate to provide care to each other. As we do so, positive neurochemical, hormonal, and organ responses ensue for both giver and receiver.

When we think of survival of our species, this makes perfect sense. No group could have made it through the relentless harshness of difficult weather and predator challenges in ancient days without some sort of cooperative and care exchange. The peer-reviewed journal *Proceedings of the Natural Academy of Sciences* has published evidence[22] that among pre-Neanderthal Pleistocene hunter-gatherers, individuals with apparent cognitive and/or physical deficits were not rejected at birth and lived to "normal" ages of the time, apparently receiving similar attention and care as other children. We are wired for care, both in the brain and in the heart.

In the forests of Poland, during those four winters, other generosities appeared. The sharing of knowledge across groups, the training of partisans by the random medically-trained person to care for wounds, breaks and illness, the huddling together in the cold and the careful apportioning of food. Orphaned children were brought under wing. Mourning was respected and the sudden findings of gifts, like a chicken or a coat, were celebrated as if there were enough for all. I'm sure kindness was not present 24/7; no doubt those fighters had to find a way to hold in check any instinct to care for oneself at the expense of another, but when the last frame of that film faded, the resounding emotion in the room was one of awe. In the darkest of moments, a spectrum of benevolence radiated.

Pet Peeves

*"I think it annoys God if you walk by the color
purple in a field and don't notice."*

—Alice Walker

My neighbor, two corners away, puts her Halloween decorations up in mid-September. This upsets me, almost as much as my other neighbor who doesn't take her Christmas lights down until April. I don't get it. I don't understand this rushing and lingering of the holiday. Can't they look at a calendar for the entire year and see that it is filled with celebration, each in its own time? And if we hurry one or hold too tight to another it jams us up against the next one, which then doesn't get its due. Like holding on to a 3rd grade friend who no longer makes sense in your life, just because they were there when you were little, which narrows the channel for new folk to enter your life, like the sweet boy in 6th grade math class who wanted to do the worksheets together. There is a rhythm to life that doesn't make sense if we are constantly hoarding a holiday or shoving it out for view way before its time.

I also have an issue with people who drive exactly the speed limit; it grates me deep into my bones, and all I want to do is literally drive up onto their bumper and help them—I use that word loosely—move along. I know I am so wrong here, I get that and one day, after I have figured out all my other ridiculously nutty attributes, I shall work on it, maybe.

My third peeve has to do with those who don't respond to texts, cards, gifts or phone calls. You all know who you are and there is no excuse for it. Our world depends on basic respectful communication, and this ghosting thing is a terribly poor behavior. Ghost a person who has done you wrong, absolutely. But not responding to someone who has sent you some form of love, that is just hurtful on so many levels.

I plan to peeve away, to vex, to gripe on about these for the rest of my days. Just so you know. Quietly. Under my breath. That's all. And maybe now and then, here, on paper.

The larger grievance, which fuels a disgruntlement I cannot ignore, is our willingness to allow stories of ill behavior, cruelty and even evil to dominate our experience. These exist and have always existed. I'm certain anthropologists have tales to tell about ancient herding peoples who exiled those who were not the same. Or tribes of nomads who were in the habit of poisoning the food of competing tribes. The earliest creation myths all have some evidence of human ignorance or malice or both, and we only need glance at any magazine that covers anything to do with the natural kingdoms to witness evidence of our greed, lust, or laziness. Still, I tell my children every single time I travel to a new country to meet with new people, there is goodness everywhere.

It is perilous to ignore evidence of our morality, generosity, and kindness. We cannot live without hope and hope lies here in the best of us.

⁓

There is a woman—Lori, Linda, Leslie, I cannot remember anything but the L of her name—who works in Africa at a nature preserve for big animals. In the brief YouTube video

I watched she narrates the tale of a young hippo, abandoned as an infant, who is brought to her preserve for survival. There are no hippos around for him to bond with, so he is placed in a large pen with baby rhinos…and the young hippo grows believing he is a rhino. This is lovely and they seem to enjoy the same opening-the-mouth-wide-and-munching-on-each-other game, and romping-around-the-enclosure game, and they sleep on the same pallet, covered in soft blankets. And all is well, except for the fact that hippos, unlike rhinos, need to spend hours a day in water so they won't burn, and as the baby hippo spends his days in the sun with his rhino brothers, his hippo-grey skin turns pink and red and inflamed. Little by little the caregiver—Lori or Lydia or Lois—has to water him with a hose and coax him into a pond which he doesn't want because none of his friends are in the pond and as we all know, when we are young, we want to be exactly where our friends are.

Baby hippos eat somewhere north of fifty pounds of grass a day—maybe as much as 80 pounds daily of grass and fruit. They are 50 to 100 pounds at birth and defecate all day long; an adult may defecate up to 400 pounds of waste a day. They are not known to be friendly as adults, and young hippos have been known to be aggressive with humans they don't know, or each other. So Linda or Layla or Luna must have to be conscious all the time as she enters the enclosure, of how fast she moves or close she gets. She must measure the rhino-hippo pod mood against her need to wash them down or nudge them to better grasses or get them medicines. She has to sight the omnipresent piles of shit, near the capering mammals, and clear them up now and then. According to my google research, Lily or Lara or Lola probably rose at 6 a.m. for the first feeding, probably does not make enough to buy a home in the US, probably has to deal often with annoying tourists or volunteers or donors who want to do good but don't understand the first thing about hippopotami or what it means to devote your life to orphaned animals.

Lauren or Lacey played with the hippo/rhino babies. She rubbed their backs, covered their bodies at night, sprayed them for fun and good skin care and watched as they found their way to a steady health. She helped the hippo, bit by bit, make a friend of a new hippo, a girl hippo, brought to the enclosure to begin to socialize the boy so that he might one day know his identity and behave in alignment with his nature, and perhaps even be re-introduced to the wild. She was patient as the two hippos began to communicate, bellowing, grunting, roaring, and felt so much joy when they became real friends and the boy began to stay in the water with his new friend for hours, just as he should, just as he needed to.

This isn't a tale of miracles or insane courage. It is one of ordinary goodness. Of the daily choice to care for a being, different and vulnerable. To choose one corner of one part of the world and make it a little more tolerable, a brighter shade of purple.

When I closed my computer, I couldn't stop thinking about the woman and her choice. She will win no prize or medal, but I hope she rests at night knowing that she has contributed something positive to our world. I hope that someone has let her know that her daily kindness is the real milk of life. With care like hers, we have a chance.

Hope, happiness, uplift are a choice. We can pay attention to the news in all its violent retelling of how awful we are and let that be the story of our living or we can balance that, mindfully balance our attention, with an active noticing of the good. It isn't hard, but it requires attention. It requires appreciation that encompasses the biggest of us and the most common, the ordinary.

Lyra, let me call her Lyra from here on, brought to us the long, perfect loveliness of the hippo, to paraphrase Galway Kinnell. She eased one heart from breaking, to steal from Emily Dickenson, and she was, as Rumi encouraged, at times a lamp and a lifeboat for the abandoned baby. She was/is the best of who any of us might be and it would take us days and days and days to count how many hours people like Lyra have been devoted to the care of others. Isn't this news worth acknowledging? A story worth sharing?

Might it be true that one of the ways any of us might contribute to our fragile future is in by reminding each other what is true within the realm of the human heart?

We are capable of so much when it comes to goodness.

I am reminded as I write this of the stories of women in war-torn refugee camps, in places far away from the café in my hometown where I come to write, who, upon noticing the orphaned children displaced with them, organize groups of "aunties" and "grandmothers" to adopt the children. With nothing but care to give, they offer all they have.

Or think now, if you will, just before you turn this page, of any time in your life when you were struggling, and ask yourself to reflect upon one gesture of help you received at that time: one bowl of food, one listening ear, a loan, a hug, a smile, the opening of a door that had been closed, or, as happened to me on the day my therapist of many years was diagnosed with brain cancer and I was told I would never see her again, the sudden appearance of lilacs on my doorstep to ease the pain.

"Nobody has ever measured, not even poets, how much the heart can hold," wrote Zelda Fitzgerald. The evidence of its infinite capacity to stretch toward each other is everywhere, even in a hippo-rhino pen, seeding a bountiful moral beauty, energetic flows of purple—lavender, iris, orchid and violet—across all our lands.

The Light Triad of Humanity

"We are challenged to change ourselves."

—Viktor Frankl

January 2021. An Austrian gentleman, Eric Schwam, having recently died at the age of 90, did the thing so many of us dream of doing. He committed an act of unheralded generosity, benefitting many. Upon his passing the city officials of Le Chambon-sur-Lignon, a French village in the southeast region of the country, received notice of the donation of approximately $2.4 million from Mr. Schwam. The gift, made in gratitude for sheltering his family from the Nazis during WWII from 1943 until the war's end, was a surprise. Little is known about Mr. Schwam, except that he and his parents survived because of the protection of the villagers in the 1940s and as a widower, without children, he made the decision to honor an entire community with his bequest.

The same morning that my partner Herb and I read about Mr. Schwam, we went outside to clear out the vegetable boxes in our garden. Just a few moments into the task, we found evidence of a bunny den, hidden underneath the layers of winter debris. Several baby bunnies (we couldn't tell exactly how many without uncovering them completely and exposing them to cold) huddled in a nest about the size of a large cereal bowl. This was the first time we'd encountered baby bunnies in our garden, and it triggered a somewhat intense conversation about sheltering vs. exposing. If we let them live there, chances are the mama would return later to share the bounty of our garden (we tend to be pretty good with lettuces) and with such a table set for her, she'd probably return to nest again the following spring.

To expose the babies seemed an impossible cruelty. It is difficult to kill a bunny with an Eric Schwam story nested in your brain.

We chose to let them be and now, as I write this a few weeks later, we have three healthy juveniles eating the tops of my irises, the lawn clover and the wildflower shoots I planted last fall. They seem happy and increasingly fat. We are also happy, though preparing for the inevitable coming battle over lettuce.

This notion of protection of young ones seems to be somehow encoded within us. About two million years ago, shared parenting within a tribe began to emerge, looking much like the network of grandparents and chosen aunties and uncles that so many of us lean on to help us raise our children. Shared sheltering enables an infant to thrive...and so, too, a species.

There is something magnificent about a village doing the same on behalf of children from another tribe. The risk so high then, and the reward only truly grasped from a moral stand-point. If Mr. Schwam and his family were to die, humanity would continue to live—three deaths an infinitesimal number in the larger context of survival, really. But were they to die, were the villagers to expose them, the moral consequences would have been annihilating.

I wish we understood this more fully at an early age. I wish this caring-for-the-other-thing was taught right next to the pile of A is for Apple cards. I wish we all thought much more about the algebra of generosity or the physics of a soul weighted by care vs. the soul empty of empathy. This is *the* science of humanity. It is the science, along with immunology and food generation, and protection of waterways, that keeps us alive. Imagine a generation of school children globally learning a shared understanding of the reciprocal nature of generosity: as we witness kindness, we are kinder in return. As we see moral excellence in action—say, the act of fairness in a complex negotiation at work—we become better organizational citizens. As we care for others, they are more likely to develop the empathy to care for strangers in return.

A positive, virtuous cycle is created in which we live into the knowing that we are never truly singular. This is the only knowing that will actually save our planet. All wellbeing, all thriving, all resilience and all survival rests in interdependence with others.

Sometimes this does seem impossible. Sometimes the odds do feel against us. School shootings. Street violence. Enslavement. Abduction. Greed. Trafficking.

But there is so much evidence in the other direction as well. So many aunties and grandfathers stepping up. So many welcoming arms opened to orphaned children. So many courageous voices holding us accountable for the highest standards of care. Researchers in the field of personality psychology have now identified the *light triad of humanity*: the three virtues that mark the best of us, exemplars of humanity across race, age, gender, socioeconomic status, geography, and time. Scott Barry Kaufman's profound work[23] enables us to see the intersection of three ways of being that mark what he terms everyday saints: Humanism (when we value and respect the dignity and worth of each individual); Faith in Humanity (belief in the fundamental goodness of humans); and Kantianism (treating others as an end unto themselves, not merely as means to our ends).

These qualities bring us to a living that is illuminated with the highest of virtues, evidenced by acts of consistent care and kindness and thoughtfulness and love, to strangers and friends alike, and even sometimes to foes.

Think of the Dalai Lama praying for the wellbeing of the Chinese. Think of Valerie Kaur reaching across prison bars to forgive the murderer of her uncle. Think of any moment you have witnessed a stranger jumping in to save someone being attacked or that one time you found yourself pumping gas near midnight and a young woman approaches you begging you for a dollar for gas and you get out of your own head, filled with doubts and judgement about how she got there or what she might buy with your money, and reach instead for your wallet, wondering, your heart filled with the impulse of Ms. Kaur and Mr. Schwam, if this one act of kindness may be the one that keeps her alive for one more night. She is, after all, someone's daughter. She does belong to someone somewhere.

It would have been quite hard to expose the baby bunnies after having read about Mr. Schwam. The luminosity of his example traveled with us into the garden...and from the light of that return, we were inspired toward our better natures. A simple example, I know. Bunnies. Lettuce. It didn't cost us much to keep them. No one and nothing really was at risk here—whether we kept them alive or exposed them, we wouldn't suffer much. Low stakes either way, for us.

All the same, having the chance to step toward goodness after reading such a story does something more than simply trigger a momentary kindness. It brings us a felt sense of what is possible. We join, if only for a day, the light-triadic-lineage of others who make real a sense that this world is worth respecting and saving. We become better.

SECTION FOUR

Fragility

"Each day, we're given many opportunities
to open up or shut down."
—Pema Chodron

The Edge of Things

"We live at the edge of the miraculous."

—Henry Miller

I have been sad for months now. A sorrow just behind the eyes. Any touch of beauty brings tears and I feel as limp as an exhausted kitten. Everywhere I look is a tender fragility and no place feels impenetrable. We are cracked and chipped and sore beyond belief. Four days ago, a 7-pound Yorkie Terrier, Macy, protected his 10-year-old owner, Lily Kwan, from a coyote attack in Toronto. Even after the predator had grabbed Macy in his mouth and shook the dog violently, even after the ripping of her back and belly, she continued to charge at the coyote and keep herself between the attacker and her owner. After spending days in the ICU, Macy will be fine—and, like the rest of the planet, not fine as well. The Northeast has been shuttered against rain, the West is a blaze of fire, while Europe is awash with floods. Like Macy, we are scarred and scared and long for respite, but putting our guard down does not feel like an option. We've moved from languishing to anguishing in hidden whispers because no one wants to quite admit that we are not—years after the official end of the Covid pandemic— better. This is the edge of things, the lip of the canyon where all below appears sharp, broken, deadly.

I don't know where to go with this pain. I often complain—disappointingly often—about having to stare a screen for eight hours a day, by myself in a home that used to feel like sanctuary. My partner leaves every day to work in our local hospital and I have been jealous of the constancy of his work, the complicated but glorious presence of his colleagues and the literal fact that he doesn't have to see the dryer, the sink, or the litter box for the bulk of his days. He is in the world of human beings trying to survive. I am trying to survive through a screen, a box that was never meant to be the primary form of love and purpose between human beings. I am at the precipice of all that I can control, looking for a self-defining dawn, to steal a phrase from poet Derek Walcott. A dawn larger than the timid light within me today. A dawn that can bless the whole of this terrifying mess and somehow bring hope.

One early morning when I was in my mid-forties, visiting friends in Vancouver, I woke early and ran a few miles to Kitsilano Bay, a waterfront that seemed to be particularly welcoming to dog owners. I watched dogs of every size take on the ocean, as their owners threw a stick or a ball into the bay. It was fun and freeing and settling to see the wet fur-shake of happy dogs and the enthusiastic love of their owners. One dog, though, a Rottie, struggled. She desperately wanted to fetch a stick. She ran circles around her owner, beg-barking for that stick to be thrown and I wondered why the owner waited. She did have a stick in her hand. She was clearly thinking about it. It felt like torture, like waiting for your father to move off his butt and get up to give you change as the ice cream truck song got farther and farther away from the end of your driveway. Finally, after perhaps three minutes of relentless pleading, the owner acquiesced and sent a stick flying. The Rottie jumped in, paddled forward maybe ten strokes, hit some inner wall of panic and turned around, a high whine from her throat, until she felt ground beneath her feet. She spun like a dervish on the transition zone of low waves and beach, in circles, barking at the stick, the owner, the ocean, and you could feel the longing, the desperate longing to be able to do something clearly beyond her ability. The owner called her back. She gave in, walked back to her owner, lay down, and in less than two minutes was up again, barking at her person to launch another stick. I watched her repeat this routine three, maybe four times, until the owner, with the kindest of hugs, told the dog "No more," and walked her away from the bay.

"Sooner or later we will come to the edge of all that we can control and find life, waiting there for us," Rachel Naomi Remen once wrote. I want to know what exactly she meant by "life." Does she mean life as in nature, butterflies, blossoms, herons rising from the ponds of our marshland? Does she mean life force as in soul, vitality, essence within us, encouraging us to go on, even as we cannot do the one lousy thing we long to do today? Or maybe the larger "life" of destiny and purpose, calling us forward toward that something that is supposed to be our thing?

It is 'sooner and later' for me, dear Rachel; I have come to the edge and I am looking to find that life thing. But as hard as I circle and bark and lean into the moment, I am lost. I cannot seem to swim and I cannot seem to let go of the pull to swim; I need a person, or an idea, to hug me and take me home—not the home I am sequestered in each and every bloody day, but someplace else, some place that makes sense in this time of frailty and fracture.

I need a home where every morning I can see the dawn, rising at the edge of day, self-defined and steady.

I know that this is a transition time, a liminal space between what had been true and normal and what isn't yet settled into normal or predictable. Everywhere, we are on the cusp of things and it is not comfortable at all; for many, it is impossible. War abounds. Violence erupts. Viruses haunt. Species die.

My experience, predominantly of advantage and safety despite its strains, is nothing compared to what others are asked to face. As the worry about safety in schools and work and community tortures us like a bad song refrain, an earworm of anxiety sounding over and over and over again, we are all on an edge of one kind or another, looking down the precipice and wondering how in God's name we will ever get from here to anywhere else intact.

At night, an image has been coming to me lately, in that shifting space between waking and sleeping. I am on an ice floe, floating in a vast ocean, and for much of the night I see no land. The currents carry me to a curve of ice-covered land, and I watch to see if the floe settles into the curve just right— to see if in fact, this is the land of my new living. But the raft of ice bumps up against the coast and is rejected. The hardened shore pushes us out, back into the swells. The ice I sit on spins again and I am carried away. I have no oar to paddle with. No compass to guide me. No stars light my way. Every night I imagine a new piece of land to settle into and each night, without fail, it is clear to me that I am unequivocally lost, unmoored and adrift.

"We live at the edge of the miraculous," wrote Henry Miller, and in this moment I call bullshit. It may be true that on the other side of this oceanic unmoored spinning, the miraculous may present itself. But in this moment of long, lingering, laborious living, Miller seems a ridiculous optimist…no different than an owner who brings her dog to water she cannot swim in, water that might in fact overwhelm her with its relentless rising depths.

I do not know how the miraculous may appear. I don't know in what form any of us may find blessing or grace or a surprise of goodness large enough to nourish our ongoing living. I am tempted, for God's sake, as a positive psychologist, to pivot here on this page right now to hope or the image of the sudden light that broke through the clouds this morning, just over the rim of Laurel Lake.

But in this very moment I seek to pause here at the edge of fear and exhaustion and despair and allow myself, in honor of all those in similar desolate borderlands, to be true to what is true. To feel all that I feel and respect the validity of these realities as well. There is never growth or forward motion in denial. If any of us seek to improve the health of our earth and its species, then we must face what is real, knowing that the capacity to hold it all—a key quality of resilience—requires the ability to not deny the consequences of a time of darkness.

Our world is bleating and bleeding, broken and in turmoil.

Every part of my being longs to make this better and that means, in this moment, to tolerate the anguish, recognize its honesty, and trust that the truth of all natural things—that nothing remains static forever—will enable one day a shift toward dawn.

Death/Reciprocity

*"The light catches in the bare branches of the maple...
The cardinal perched near the top of the tree bursts into
radiance, into flame, and for that moment nothing matters
at all—not the still soil nor the clattering branches nor
the way this redbird will fall to the ground in time, a cold
stone, and I too will grow cold, and all my line."*

—Margaret Renkl

This morning a juvenile black bear crossed through the yard. He has done so often this summer, once lying fully on his back, belly and pelvis splayed open to the sun as he scratched away at the stings of summer. I videoed him from the back porch, less than 10 yards distant. He clearly had no fear of predators, and I knew that my stillness wouldn't endanger me. We don't bother about the bears much here. They are vegetarians at heart and seem most interested in human things when there is access to soup or pie near an open window. If we are mindful, we can notice the growth in their width, the confidence in their gait with a sense of ease. The babies leave their mothers, it seems, just about the time the sun is at its height here in the northeast and their frolicking manner shifts to a more serious approach. The days are spent foraging and they cross through the yards in a loop of trails that lead eventually to the gentle mountains across the way. In a year's time, new babies arrive, and I find myself wondering about their lineages and the traceline of knowledge that brings them to the same trails and backyard pathways each summer. To me they look the same, but they cannot possibly be. Nature has its way with each of the living, the clock inevitably ticking in one direction only.

Beauty is miraculous, in part, because it is transitory. Disintegration is built into the very DNA of all living things. It is a profound truth to accept; there is no fixed permanent state in nature. Even the most long-lived organic creatures— the Galapagos tortoise of a few centuries or the Great Basin bristlecone pine of Nevada, thought to be over 5,000 years old— will eventually pass. All will grow cold, as Margaret Renkl[24] reminds us, and it is this certainty that informs the intensity of what we find beautiful. Some part of us, with at least some conscious awareness, is primed to know that even the hardiest elements of the natural kingdoms will break down; nothing remains as it has been. Each viewing, each moment of noticing brings with it its own inevitable fray.

The same is also true, I suspect, of excellence and goodness. What is excellent in one era, in one location, fades with progress and innovation (think flip phone or horse-drawn carriage). Goodness has impact in its moment, and it sometimes lives forward into emerging timelines. Anne Frank, Nelson Mandela, Mother Theresa, Viktor Frankl come to mind. However, like the beings that carry that goodness, much decency disappears with the forgetful forward push of time into the future; our acts hold value for but a generation or two.

Collapse is built into our bones.

From one lens, a kaleidoscopic turn to the side of the final-ity of death, this can be seen as a kindness. Little new can be sustained in any garden without the decay of the layers laid down before. Failing the natural disintegration of things, the old would choke the new. It is a generosity, this fragility, as well as a sorrow. Without mortality we might not know the preciousness of this life we have been given. Each bear would bring no new surprise. Each morning would be a repetition that might bring tedium. How often have we found ourselves resenting the continuity of our days, only to have that pre-dictability torn asunder by disease, divorce, death…and with that tearing a poignant appreciation arises for what had been lost, even in its expectedness. We love what we find beautiful. We protect and elevate goodness and we do so because of an awareness of its fleeting presence. Every daisy is the same, and yet no daisy will bow for more than one summer.

In the pain of loss, it can be hard to remember this hidden generosity of passing, leaving room for those to come. Jungian therapist and global storytelling force Clarissa Pinkola Estes observes "a gentle truth of our lives here on planet Earth: In a meaningful life, we are ever on our way to death and ever on our way to new life again."

Two inseparable forces at play, perhaps the most influential, paradoxical AND of our reality: we live, and as we do so, we decay.

But let's pause here for a moment, mid-cycle, if you will. Let's rest into the AND for a time and see the hidden generosity there a bit more closely. We are living and dying at the same time. All natural forces rise and fall. Yet the AND, this powerful connector between two seemingly opposing elements, is actually a doorway into how we might engage with this temporary aspect of beauty and goodness in such a way that we become more fully engaged in a life-generating pattern. I'm speaking here about an ordinary, daily, backyard kind of decency that is always possible—that of reciprocity. In the AND of every moment, we have an opportunity to engage in three general ways: a) as if we are the only thing that matters; b) as if nothing matters; and c) as if our place in the world matters just as much as the world and its inhabitants matter.

From this third pathway we might engage in our life/death/ life reality in a generative, beneficent and life-giving way.

In her book *Braiding Sweetgrass*, Robin Wall Kimmerer illustrates this third way through her tale of the simple strawberry. She reflects that wild strawberries appear as an unexpected gift, an unearned reward. And our choice—the one that will sustain our species and our world—is to behave as if the strawberry is not only a gift, but an invitation into reciprocity, the generosity of the berry becoming a trigger for continued kindness. She picks the berries with appreciation, brings them to her father (who loves them dearly) for his birthday, a gift of sweetness as well as attention. In doing so, she honors the berry and her father, and her kindness brings out a further generosity—the love on his face, a reflection of the happiness she has brought him. She writes: "Gifts from the earth or from each other establish a particular relationship, an obligation of sorts to give, to receive, and to reciprocate. The field gave to us, we gave to my dad, and we tried to give back to the strawberries." She gives back by honoring the miracle of the plant, and respecting its natural cycles of harvest, and perhaps in an equally impactful way by sharing with us the stories of the importance of being in a mutual reciprocal relationship with the berry and her kind.

She continues: "Our human relationship with strawberries is transformed by our choice of perspective. It is human perception that makes the world a gift. When we view the world this way (through the lens of reciprocity) strawberries and humans alike are transformed. The relationship of gratitude and reciprocity thus developed can increase the evolutionary fitness of both plant and animal." (Kimmerer, *Braiding Sweetgrass*, 25–27).

And here is what I suggest: embracing this notion of reciprocity, seeing the natural kingdoms through the lens of appreciation, enables us to accept that AND of living and dying within a regenerative cycle. Our appreciation for beauty, goodness, and excellence does not stop time in the largest sense, but it does bring a pause to the inevitable decline that time brings—a pause that creates a forward motion for new patterns of generosity and abundance to emerge. It is as if we might actually become larger than the force of our mortality by being a force of return to our world. We become consonant with the natural cycle that has enabled centuries of life in such a way that we do not destroy, we enhance. We do not harm, we heal.

Soon the black bear will disappear into a burrow or cave. I'll watch the ground grow brown, the summer delphiniums and phlox fade into thin grey stalks. I'll bring in the outdoor chairs, the sun umbrellas and glass balls I've hidden in the garden. When we return them in the coming spring, I'll look for the bear's return and I probably won't see exactly him, but if I am lucky, and we often are here, I'll see a momma bear and her tumbling little ones romp through the yard, scenting the trail of their forebears, carrying their species forward.

We have been gifted so much.

It takes so little effort to see the world with an appreciative lens and there is so much return in this gaze. Wherever you are, surrounded by concrete or palm, by forest or plain, beauty surrounds, goodness rises, and excellence stands tall. The headlines may be dark. Evil does exist. So much needs our care. And yet...we can still steward the world into health, bit by bit, grateful and generous for each moment we can choose to make a difference.

There is no greater call. There is no time but now.

The Death Book

If I should die soon...and I will...
Know that joy came to me often.
The red fox turned toward me yesterday
In the field just past the beaver pond
And waited till I could see the gold gleam
Beading the burnt orange of her fur. She
Held my glance as if to say, "There you are!"
and a smile, I swear, was offered.
How often the world spoke to me.
How often the wind listened and the eagles
Descended at the right moment to remind me
Of all the impossible graces.

—Maria Sirois

Sometimes, in my hybrid working world, I do not jump out of bed. I linger. On those mornings when I don't have to be present right away to the zoom call or the staff meeting, I hang out amidst the bed sheets and the righteous cat and imagine what I will add to my death book. I linger because I can— no one else is home these days and my guy is off to work for approximately two more years. Once he retires, I am aware that my lingering days will be numbered. He is the action figure in our relationship; I am the thought bubble cloud of words and questions and wonderings. And I linger because, within the narrows of my ever-so-intense psyche, I have a sneaking suspicion that all is not as it should be and the habits of living that brought me to this age, mostly with health and sense of purpose intact, are no longer the solid pillars they once were.

Something within me is afoot—a hint of doubt that I can keep going on as I have been, without having to re-cohere my place in the world.

The pandemic altered things. It is as if I am a ticking watch with a faulty second hand, not quite on time, not quite up to par, not quite as certain of the exactness of coordinates within. I am neither languishing or anguishing but something like dissembling.

This is not a bad thing...I think. It has happened before, when the world before no longer tilted on the same axis and I had to find my way to a new normal. It is disorienting. So I linger in the cool sheets...and consider my death book.

This is a book I haven't actually created or even started a file on. It's more of an idea than a book, a sketch of a notion of what I want my children to most know about my life. It will answer the big questions of course: where my will is stashed, who holds the keys to the lock box, which passwords open which accounts, and how long they are to wait before pulling the plug should I become brain dead: four seconds—one to honor each of the directions of life on this planet—the north of sky, the south of earth, the east of the ocean lying against our Massachusetts coast, and the west of mountains.

The book should have some indication of the bigger wisdom gained through my living, right? I should leave them with the crucial guidelines that have enabled my sanity or at least my endurance in tending sanity. Important tidbits like, "When the shit hits the fan it really does help to clean a dish or wash a towel...some days we can only control what we can control within the square of our living," or "Cats lie…they act all purry and sweet when you've been away but the second you feed them, they place you back in the category of things-to-be-tolerated if not outright ignored. This is not love. This is strategy."

They will need to know things and I ought to list them. Because it is what every child wants, I am sure, motherisms coming their way from beyond whatever ground site on which I've instructed them to scatter my ashes.

I would like my ashes to be near a tree. That will be made clear. A tree that is neither young nor old but has a bit of years left in her.

A tree in a forest of trees.

A tree of community and belonging.

One that hikers will pass by, and small children will touch, and happy little animals will scamper upon. A tree that touches both earth and sky, so she cannot be too short, cowering under the canopy of others, but neither must she be giant. We have but a few giants in the northeast and she need not be one of the rare ones. Just a tree, in a wood, where others grow.

I will try, in the book, to represent how much this Earth meant to me. How, though I chose a living of word and story and teaching, the flow of ideas was only made possible because of the lands that offered their magnanimous arms and the animals that shared those lands so abundantly. I have been granted a kingdom, truly, a sovereignty of bounty, and from that kingdom, a vitality of sustaining hope. I have found in the mountains and farmlands and watercourses of the east, friendship and delight.

Cultural historian and priest Thomas Berry was asked to share words for a future generation, in anticipation of his passing. He wrote, "Our existential questions must now be: How do we relate to the earth and to the universe? Our most basic issue is how we bond with the earth... tell them they will meet great companions along the way, including those that burrow in the soil, fly in the air and swim in the sea..."[25]

Just like Thomas Berry, I have met great companions.

Once four red fox appeared in my yard, just as the dawn was emerging. My children were babies, sleep was erratic, and I found myself downstairs, staring out the window at the waking day just as two pairs of foxes entered the yard. They paused to sit as if to take in the warming rays and looked directly at my living room window. It is hard to say if they could see through the glass, but it certainly felt like they could. They held my gaze and I held theirs and in the brief seconds of that hold I knew again a sense of sustaining kinship.

It is in such moments of our lives that meaning arises. For me it has been in the startling moments of encounters with the natural kingdoms that a sense of significance and endurance has grown.

Berry continued, "Tell them [future generations] to seek their own role in the larger evolutionary process: tell them that humans are always in the process of becoming, always "opening to greater life," if they can learn to see it. Above all, tell them to practice an intimate presence to the beauty and wonder of the natural world through their intuitive awareness that recognizes the oneness of all life; tell them to stop and enlarge moments throughout their days to become aware of the mysteries and miracles of creation all around them— the movement of a squirrel, the sound of a bird, the pattern of a leaf, changing patterns of light, the sun, the rain, the stars, dawn and sunset. Tell them we are not ourselves without everything and everyone else."

We are not ourselves without everything and everyone else. Only when we practice that intimate presence to the beauty around and within us do we move closer to the most important understanding of this time: Our world will not survive without each of us developing a clarity of purpose to protect that world as best we can.

Beauty and wonder are available, through memory if not immediacy, every day and through their appreciation we become connected to a sense of larger livings that inspire and elevate us.

As we model the practice of noticing beauty and excellence in all its forms, we not only become kinder human beings, we shape human behavior in the direction of positive action.

We cannot do everything, but we can do much in one lifetime to change the territories near us and influence those on a farther shore.

I cannot imagine the moment of my dying—the anticipated pain on the faces of my loved ones is enough to shut down that storyline within a heartbeat. What I can bring forward is a sense that if I have contributed to the living that was mine to touch, they will know that there are pathways of hope and change open through the smallest of actions. It may not seem like much to notice the gleam of a fox or the fire of the eagle's glance and share that noticing…it is not much, and it is everything.

We need each other.

We are ourselves, with each other.

We are not alone in our living.

We never have been.

Now is the time for each of us to live as if this were true.

SECTION FIVE

Practices

"Sometimes the simplest move keeps sorrow from being the only person living in the house."

—Naomi Shihab Nye

Daily Practices

"One touch of nature makes the whole world kin."

—*William Shakespeare*

Morning Time

Each morning for two weeks, find a spot where you might rest quietly for a moment or two. For that moment, take in the beauty that most feeds your soul that day. Might it be a color? A poem? A scent? Allow yourself to begin your day in serenity and appreciation, as if each day were an offering to nourish you. As if each morning, just as it was, might become a template for how to live an entire day, and from that understanding, how we might live a life.

Day Time

For one week, journey out into your day, photographing (or drawing) something that you find beautiful. Look for patterns that take your breath away. Natural artifacts appearing in ordinary ways that suddenly seem miraculous. The angle of a thing. The mathematics of fern. The red of a newt against a moss-covered log. Or the corner of the note your child left you in fifth grade, curled and torn now, stuffed into the back of that drawer you are finally cleaning out—the corner that simply says, 'go to bech to,' meaning: "will you go to the beach with me too?" At the end of the week, gather the images you have created, and notice how much your days offer.

Twilight Time

Set your alarm for a three-minute break at the time you consider liminal…that time between light and dark, afternoon and evening, day's end and night's beginning. Close the door at work or find a corner, shutter the window of your room, and for three minutes bring a memory of beauty or goodness or excellence to mind, a memory that continues to inspire you and nurture you. Invite the fullness of the memory in and notice, in just a few moments, the change in your body's energy and your mood. Practice for two weeks.

Evening Time

For thirty nights, just before you close your eyes for sleep, record the one thing you have found beautiful in the day. It could take the form of physical beauty, or an experience of excellence, or of moral goodness…just one thing that for that day meant you were touched by beauty. At the end of the month, review your notes, looking for patterns, for unique moments recorded, for forms of beauty that seem to matter the most to you at this time. And notice how this has changed you. Who have you now become with this practice?

Micro Practices

*"What you do every day matters more than
what you do once in a while."*

—Gretchen Rubin

The One Corner Practice

For 7 days, for a few moments only, choose one corner of your space to make more beautiful. Dust the cobweb. Trim the dead plant leaves. Wash the dish. Toss the debris. Add a ribbon to the windowsill. Change the lightbulb. Or look to the corners within: Ten deep breaths. One prayer. Massage that one muscle. Little by little we find our way to a more beautiful living by bringing a clean energy to our home and the home within. To keep sorrow or anger or doubt from being the only energy of the home, we can cultivate the habit of tiny daily shifts that add just a bit more to the beauty around and within.

The Texting-as-if-Texting-Actually-Mattered Practice

For ten days in a row, choose one person to text. You could choose someone different each day or the same person. Send them a picture of beauty or text reminding them of the ways in which you find them beautiful. Pair this with a ritual or habit already in place (that morning cup of coffee or late afternoon walk) and do so without expectation in return. See if for just one second you might become a light to another and notice how your experience of living changes ten days later.

Words that Heal

For thirty mornings, or thirty evenings, I encourage you to pick up your phone. First thing in the morning, last thing at night. From the landscape of the internet find a quote, a line, a poem, a lyric, a language that soothes your soul. Something that, as you read the words to yourself, offers an encouragement or a healing. Let the news of the day fade. Allow the strains to disappear and the to do list to rest upon the nightstand where it will remain, faithfully, while you seek solace in the territory of writing. Keep a list...label it what you will. I call mine The Beauty Well. And return to the well as often as you need throughout the day. Share your findings with trusted souls or keep them within the temple of your body. Let them be as a mantra or a prayer, however you need them. Invite them in...you are not alone.

Weekly Practices

"What you encounter, recognize or discover depends to a large degree on the quality of your approach...When we approach with reverence, great things decide to approach us. Our real life comes to the surface and its light awakens the concealed beauty in things."

—John O'Donohue

Savoring

Plan a moment in your weekly calendar to travel, either in person, or in your mind's eye, to a place of natural beauty. Allow yourself to remain there for 20 minutes. Notice all that you see, feel, hear in this place. Notice how your body responds to the beauty you have chosen. Savor this moment as deeply as you can. If your mind wanders, that is okay. Simply notice the wandering, say 'oh well' and return to your absorption in beauty.

Seeking

What are those small moments, that bring a chill to your being? An elegant turn of phrase? A chord of music? A stranger holding the door for another? The hummingbird hover? Enter your week with eyes wide open for a moment—just one—when you felt that sense of being transported beyond yourself with wonder and appreciation. Record the moment and do so for each of four weeks. Notice what happens when awe becomes a pattern in your living. See how it might enable your love of this world, your endurance, your capacity to reach out and touch another.

Signaling

Whenever human beings meet and greet each other the possibility for moral goodness exists. Our work environments, whether at home via the computer, or in person, create an opportunity for us to witness goodness in action, and to elevate and emulate that goodness as to signal to others of its value. Why not become the one who brings the best of us to the table? Why not become the lighthouse of the team, reflecting back to the team a moment each week, that demonstrated the best of those who carry the work of your organization forward? Why not choose to allow work to become a temple, a sanctuary, a hall of the best of yourself? What truly do you have to lose?

School Practices
(for Educators and Students)

"Attention to Beauty and Excellence is a compass, heading us in directions that make a profound positive difference."

—*Justin Robinson*

Conversations That Matter

Imagine a moment in school, when you halt the teaching of curricula and infuse a conversation that will change the course of the day. You ask simply this: "What, despite the bad things that happen, do you find beautiful in our world?" A conversation centered on attention to beauty in any form. Perhaps you offer this as an essay prompt, or a discussion moment. Perhaps you ask the little ones to draw an image or cut out pictures that remind them. Maybe it becomes a quarterly moment, or a shared exploration with another class. You might offer an evening event for the school, in which your students present their offerings. Imagine how you might change the tenor of your class, the tone of the school.

The Happening of Health All Around Us

Climate change anxiety continues to rise for adolescents globally. The antidote to anxiety rests in positive action and in gathering evidence of positive change, both of which soothe and elevate hope. Might it be possible to invite students to consider examining evidence of healing that has happened for the planet? The return of wolves to the wild? The birth of new coral beds? The healing of the ozone layer? This might be done as an ecological afterschool group, a history assignment, or a writing assignment. Consider: where has a literal repair of the world happened and how might that cascade into greater repair?

Heroes, Heroines and Wonderful People Everywhere

Wherever one looks, when one looks with an appreciative eye, a story of goodness makes itself known. A quarterly offering of a school, or in one classroom, might shift the lens of attention of students to sharing stories of exemplars, of hidden heroes and heroines within one's family, or of regular people in our communities who do much to hold the fabric of goodness and excellence together. Story elevates, inspires, and integrates learning from multiple disciplines at the same time. Moreover, it offers any student a chance to experience a sense of awe without having to travel to the farther reaches of the world. Here, in fact, is how we bring the world closer. Here is how we bridge divides and remind those under our care of their connectedness to the best of human beings throughout the planet.

The Best of Us: The Cabinet of Excellence

There is an elegant beauty to science equations, a lyrical beauty to math, a pulsing beauty to the ability of a musician to land a note with the right tone at the right time. Excellence occurs in every domain. Educators who have integrated positive psychology practices find themselves often marveling at the excellence of performance, of endurance, of learning agility, of achievement, in addition to excellence of character. We might choose to bring this to a classroom, creating a literal or metaphoric "Cabinet of Excellence" where work is celebrated, not only for its extraordinariness of content, but for its inherent elegance, refinement, finesse, or delicate subtlety.

Being Beauty/Excellence

"The most beautiful people we have known are those who have known defeat, known suffering...and have found their way out of the depths. These persons have an appreciation, a sensitivity, and an understanding of life that fills them with compassion... Beautiful people do not just happen."

—Elisabeth Kubler-Ross

Being

This is a practice of self-study, of recognition of the beauty within you, exactly as you are and have always been. Choose a journal that feels just right. Find a pen or marker that sits perfectly in your hand, or open a page on your laptop and give it a name that only you can fully appreciate. Find your way into a space of appreciation for yourself, for 30 days, journal about the evidence of your beauty—the shape of your palm, the generosity of your spirit, the way your mouth curves unevenly, but broadly when you smile. Allow room for the quirkiness of your essence; that which you find so lovely even if others do not. This is a practice of kindness too, of quieting the voices that seek to demean us or limit our celebration. And for those with a deep humility, who are most comfortable not seeking a spotlight or recognition or pridefulness, please note that as we honor who we are and what we have been given, we become more benevolent human beings.

Becoming

Consider, over a few days' time, the exemplars of moral goodness who most inspire you. Pick 3–5 exemplars. Choose exemplars from various realms, perhaps one from your personal realm, one from community or work, one from the larger world, one from history, etc. Take note of what it is about them, their characters or values, their actions, their contributions. See if you can excavate some of the qualities that you would most like to emulate. List the top two qualities—the ones that feel most easily accessible to you and the most inspiring. For the next two weeks consider this as a morning inquiry: What would it be like to activate that quality today just 5% more? We are practicing the art of becoming...of shaping who we are by shaping ourselves in the direction of who we might become. Notice how it feels to amplify this quality, to consciously choose to activate the better parts of ourselves.

Burnishing

To burnish is to polish, to make shine, to cause to gleam or sparkle. Every one of us has qualities that are necessary and wonderful. Qualities of inherent goodness and beauty that others admire—patience, or that easy laugh, a listening presence or skill with a brush. What would it be like to spend a week, being who you are, behaving as you do, but this time, for this week, choosing to bring that skill or attribute in unexpected ways? See if you might extend the quality in a new direction or bring it to bear in a novel manner. See in other words how very big you might become within yourself in the ways that already benefit our world.

Repair of the World Practices

"Ritual...opens a crack for the sacred to enter."

—*Gretchen Legler*

The Long Road Back to Better

Coral reefs spawn but once a year. Pacific salmon are semelparous, meaning that after spawning once, all the adults die. Female elephants may be able to breed up to three times a year, but once pregnant, carry for an average of 18–22 months. Ensuring the survival of species such as these is a long game, with many potential hazards along the way. The protracted road back to a world of eco-health and specie-specific robustness requires perseverance and a focused attention. A gorgeous practice: identify one specie you would want to benefit. Decide to plant a flag in the ground on behalf of this one kind of tree, or animal, or flying being. Inform your people. Participate as you can in the recovery or ongoing health of that specie over the remainder of your lifetime. Keep your focus invigorated by surrounding yourself by images of the particular beauty that can only be known by that creature or that plant. Search for the ways in which the eagle or the sloth has developed excellence in survival, mating, or feeding skills. Become intimately related— Taylor Swift and her cats, Monet and his water lilies, Craig Foster and his kelp forests—as if your legacy depended upon your ability to witness, care and steward the wellbeing of this one specific particle of life.

Loving Kindness in the Gardens of the World

"The garden of the world has no limits except in your mind. Its presence is more beautiful than the stars, with more clarity than the polished mirror of your heart," wrote Rumi. Mindful appreciation of the gardens in front of us calms the mind, soothes the heart and strengthens the will. Might we return to those gardens with more than just our gaze, but the energy of kindness? What might happen if we were to seat ourselves near a flower bed, a vegetable patch, a stand of pines and infuse the very land of their roots with metta-meditations? Might we not experience more than just the temporary awareness of loveliness? Perhaps a layering of compassion would arise such that we might pull a weed now and then, or nurture the soil. I wonder if we might discover within ourselves more than longing and kindness, but a protectiveness that inspires us to share that beauty and say something about its necessary and potent gifts. And too, in a weekly ritual of loving kindness mediation we would find ourselves with a gentler garden within, a quieting of the angers or despairs that have brought suffering to our heart, and a rising of the blossoms of goodness and hope.

The Photo-Journal Project*

For 14 days take a photo of some aspect of the world you find beautiful, and if you are bound to home, take a photo of a photo found on the web of beauty in your world. Line your room with these photos. Notice what means the most to you about them, and why they inspire you so. Allow their impact to take hold. Then, tell one person, just one person, about this impact and how this beam of beauty betters your life. Ask them to do the same: 14 days of images of beauty, sharing them in return with someone else. Make a chain of beauty images across your net. Without fanfare or strain, the chain itself will inspire action. Positive action has a contagion effect, and we can contribute to that effect from our neighborhoods.

Inspired by the work of professor and researcher and awesome human, Dr. Michael Steger.

A Final Note

"Go forward with courage."

—*Chief White Eagle*

My first writing teacher, the late Michelle Gillett, whom I adored, once asked me, when I handed her a sheaf of half-written stories, fragments that seemed linked to me, but as yet made no sense as a whole, "What is the one thing you want the reader to know or to see?" And I've used that question as a guidepost in the shaping of all my writing and storytelling since. Here, then, is the one thing I wish for each of you to know after reading these pages (and thank you, thank you, thank you for doing so):

If we choose to shape how we see so that we more often include beauty, excellence and goodness, and if we choose to then share what we see, we will not only be happier, kinder, and more often inspired, we will, more likely than not, take action to protect some small corner of our world. In so doing, we become active participants in the cause of sustaining life itself. We steward the future, a better future, bit by tiny bit. And we grant our young ones the possibility of an Earth that continues to be a vital, vibrant home.

I know that this, when considered through the lens of realities that are often daunting and excruciating, may seem a "tomorrow task," or a "for-someone-else-who-has-it-easier" task, and I know that we may find ourselves overwhelmed by how very much ought to be cleaned up, studied, harbored, cared for, and/or adopted. And yet I also know, in every fiber of my being, that it is never too late to begin and that no action, no matter how small, is insignificant.

Every action creates an energy of potential further goodness.

Beauty, excellence, and goodness are generative—they create more of the same.

Right now, two people I love are struggling to find work. A student of mine has received her second cancer diagnosis. Dementia has taken hold of a dear friend, addiction another, and just last week I attended the funeral of my cousin's wife, who died unexpectedly and young. War abounds, hate exists. We use and abuse each other. The list of critically endangered species is nearly 10,000 and every day so many of us fear that we will lose the last living unique expression of life in some form. The world's assaults continue, there is no denying this. But I have a choice. We have a choice. Become a bit more of a light on behalf of humanity and our earth...or not.

A thousand years ago, when I was 12, I took my yellow ten-speed, built-for-boys bike right out the driveway, left onto Crooked Street, and left into the driveway of the ranch house that bordered the fields behind our newish-development. Leaving the house on a weekend afternoon was customary at that time, after chores were done of course. This was in the early 1970s when dogs ran free and we, all the kids in the neighborhood, were subject to the same mantra each day from our non-helicopter, non-snowplow parents, "Go outside and play."

Summer days and nights were kickball, wiffleball, four-square, and walks in the creek that cut through my street. Just like in the town of my birth, all the moms and dads in this new town seemed to know all the kids and whenever a parent stepped outside onto the front steps and yelled for one of us, we had an unspoken contract to let that kid know that it was time to head in.

And then one day, I took my bike and went right.

Left was the center of the neighborhood where Kay and Jeff and Kathy and Linda and all those parents lived. Right was unknown.

At that age, riding the edge of longings that pulled me out of my house, I remember needing something new…something that didn't include the gang or my brothers or the constant press to be a part of a group. So, without telling anyone, I went right and then left and cut through the driveway, where I had spied a small path a few weeks prior. I rode my bike into the fields, pedaling onto the path that I would later understand to be a deer trail. At 12 I didn't know that deer walked tracks each season between the hills we had tamed for our houses. That day it looked exactly like a trail just for me, just big enough for a girl and her bike. I rode the path about 80 yards and followed it up a rise bending deeper into the field and away from the houses. At the top of the rise, the land opened in front of me—acres of meadow that hadn't been cultivated. Queen Anne's lace brushed against my ankles, and I could see the rampant dandelions amidst grasses and waving stalks of weeds I could not name. The path took me down the rise, through the fields, warm now by the sun, and into a quiet place.

I rode for about 10 minutes, wheels whooshing against the brush, small bits of rock bouncing off the bike. At the top of yet another small rise I paused. The air was still, even as insects buzzed nearby. The sun's beams lightened everything, and the sky held a steady blue. No animal appeared or mysterious figure. No swooping eagle or animal totem, no ram's horn call or trumpet of angels...and yet...a blessing visited me then. A grace. I have no other word for it.

In the field, in the yellow-white light of summer, I felt seen and known.

Not by a presence but by the land itself. As if the ground and the hills and the trail had been waiting for me to show in this way on that day. As if every moment of cleaning dishes or waiting my turn at bat had prepared me to stop and feel, for the first time, alive, grounded, a part of life itself and life a part of me. My being thrummed with a gentle but certain strum of vibration—I could feel my own life force as clear as water rushing through our creek and in that sensation, I sensed love, a force of affection from me and to me and from the land and to the land. The land suddenly existed not as a place from which to stand or sit or run on top of but as an entity unto its own—and a being, a vital being that was neither me nor separate from me.

It is so hard to put words to what is nearly ineffable.

A communion, a closeness and intimacy with the land and the living of that land, occurred to me then. Even as I looked at the very plainness of the field, the grasses and weeds, I sensed such a depth of import and worth that being alive became a matter of significance. And the very punch of that aliveness embodied in a field—that still, radiating, natural beauty—caused me to feel deeply and powerfully and vibrantly not alone, not unimportant, not bereft.

A Blackfoot warrior, Crowfoot, was once thought to have said, "Hold onto what is good. Even if it is a handful of earth." May we each find a way to do so.

He continued, "Hold on to what you must do, even if it's a long way from here…Hold on to my hand, even if someday I'll be gone away from you."

I am holding on.

To the ground of our earth.

To the awake ones who have seen and cared for beauty and goodness in all its forms.

To the hands of those who have come before and called out the wonder of our living.

And now, to you.

Resources Cited

Introduction

1   Diessner & Niemiec. (2022). "Can Beauty Save the World? Appreciation of Beauty Predicts Proenvironmental Behavior and Moral Elevation Better Than 23 Other Character Strengths." August 2022, *Ecopsychology* 15 (2).

An Important Note About this Book

2   Peterson, C., & Seligman, M. E. P. (2004). *Character strengths and virtues: A handbook and classification*. Oxford University Press; American Psychological Association.

Section One: Beauty

3   Wheatley, M. (2024). Practices to Awaken Generosity, Creativity, and Kindness in Ourselves and Our Organizations. Berrett-Koehler Publishers; California.

4   Capaldi, C. A., Passmore, H.-A., Nisbet, E. K., Zelenski, J. M., & Dopko, R. L. (2015). "Flourishing in nature: A review of the benefits of connecting with nature and its application as a wellbeing intervention." *International Journal of Wellbeing*, 5(4), 1-16.

5   Sifferlin, Alexandra. (July 14, 2016). "The Healing Power of Nature," *Time*. https://time.com/4405827/the-healing-power-of-nature/.

6   Dillard, A. (1974). *Pilgrim at Tinker Creek*. Harper Collins; New York, New York.

7   Delistraty, Cody, C. (2014). "The Beauty-Happiness Connection." *The Atlantic*. https://www.theatlantic.com/health/archive/2014/08/the-beautyhappiness-connection/375678/.

8   Tippett, Krista. (2022). "The Inner Landscape of Beauty." On Being Podcast. https://onbeing.org/programs/john-odonohue-the-inner-landscape-of-beauty/.

9   Keltner, Dacher. (2023). *Awe: The New Science of Everyday Wonder and How It Can Transform Your Life*. Penguin Press; New York.

Section Two: Excellence

10   Anderson, Sam. (2016). David's Ankles: How Imperfections Could Bring Down the World's Most Perfect Statue. *New York Times*. Aug. 17, 2016.

11   McCord, Joan. (2007). *Crime and Family: Selected Essays*. Temple University Press; Philadelphia.

12   Boy, Jeremy, and Gluecker, Andreas. (July 2, 2020). "Positive Deviance: Positive Outliers Matter." https://www.undp.org/policy-centre/singapore/blog/positive-deviance-positive-outliers-matter.

13   Ritchie, Hannah. (April, 2023). "Are We the Last Generation or the First Sustainable One?" https://www.ted.com/talks/hannah_ritchie_are_we_the_last_generation_or_the_first_sustainable_one?language=en.

14   Miller, Caroline Adams. (2017). *Getting Grit: The Evidence-Based Approach to Cultivating Passion, Perseverance, and Purpose*. Sounds True, Boulder, Colorado.

15   Lusseyran, Jacques, and Cameron, Elizabeth. (2006). *And There Was Light*. Second Edition. Morning Light Press; Idaho.

16   Doerr, Anthony. (2014). *All the Light We Cannot See*. Scribner; New York.

17   Limon, Ada. (2015). *Bright Dead Things*. Milkweed Editions; Minnesota.

18   Kimmerer, Robin Wall. (2013). *Braiding Sweetgrass: Indigenous Wisdom, Scientific Knowledge and the Teachings of Plants*. Milkweed Editions; Canada.

Section Three: Moral Beauty (Goodness)

19   Carson, Rachel. (1962). *Silent Spring*. Houghton Mifflin; Boston.

20   Lyubormirsky, Sonya. (2010). *The How of Happiness*. Piatkus Books; London.

21   McGonigal, Kelly. (2016). *The Upside of Stress: Why stress is good for you, and how to get good at it*. Penguin; New York.

22   Hublin, Jean-Jacques. (April 21, 2009). *The Prehistory of Compassion. Proceedings of the National Academy of Sciences of the United States of America*. Vol. 106-16.

23   Kaufman, Scott Barry. (March 11, 2019). "The Light vs. Dark Triad of Personality: Contrasting Two Very Different Profiles of Human Nature." *Frontiers in Psychology*: Vol. 10-2019.

Section Four: Fragility

24   Renkl, Margaret. (2019). *Late Migrations: A Natural History of Love and Loss.* Milkweed Editions; Canada.

25   Toben, Carolyn, W. (2012). *Recovering a Sense of the Sacred: Conversations with Thomas Berry*. Timberlake Earth Sanctuary Press; North Carolina.

Acknowledgments

Jenne Young sat with me for days upon days in our local café, working quietly on her work as I wrote this book. It is the best form of parallel play I know, two friends, side by side, allowing all the space one needs to focus, with only the briefest of interruptions to check in on life outside of writing and sip a coffee or two. Thank you, Jenne, for all those wonderful days.

My father, through his father, inspired my love of the woods, and my mother, my love of flowers, and so I knew my way into an appreciation of natural beauty from my early days. That love only grew as I became introduced to the writers, poets and thinkers who have opened the eyes of many to beauty in its myriad forms, including the exquisite nature of excellence. I've honored many here in this work and my debt to them is limitless.

I exist in a field of kindness. To my dear friends who listened to me talk about my beauty book as an idea for years and then held me through its various iterations and explanations— thank you. I owe you relentless streams of gin and chocolate.

To my writing teacher, mentor and inspiring human, Phyllis Theroux, who, when I told her I wanted to write about beauty gave me the best advice, "Keep it focused. Keep it small." And she was a 1,000 percent right. Beauty in the abstract is impossibly large. Beauty bounded by a lens enables us to relate enough to enter its field, while sensing the huge, glorious array of themes it offers.

To Jesse, Raphaela and the Krantrois clan—I am deeply inspired by how you each find ways to love your lives, and the furry ones, even with a surround of global brokenness.

And to Herb, you are goodness incarnate. I am blessed beyond words to have your love.

About the Author

Maria Sirois, Psy.D., is a resilience expert, positive psychologist and international consultant, known for her authenticity, wisdom and compassion. She has spent more than three decades by the bedsides of the dying, in the boardrooms of business executives, and everywhere in-between, offering data, stories, tools and perspectives that enable us to cultivate resilience, health, wisdom and a greater capacity to lead ourselves and others well, no matter the strain or suffering of the moment. She is the author of two other books: *A Short Course in Happiness After Loss (And Other Dark, Difficult Times)* and *Every Day Counts*. Find her at mariasirois.com.

www.ingramcontent.com/pod-product-compliance
Lightning Source LLC
Chambersburg PA
CBHW021104130626
46554CB00002B/524